UTAH

UTAH BY ROAD

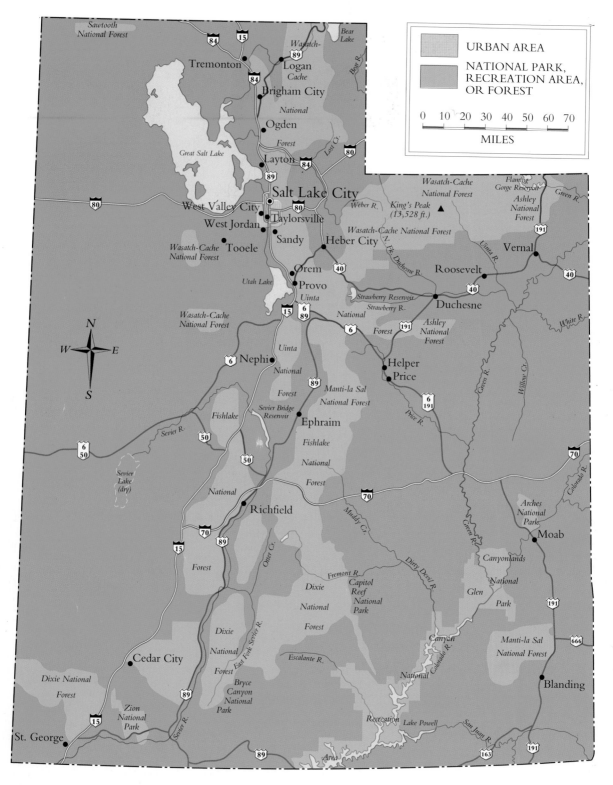

URBAN AREA

NATIONAL PARK, RECREATION AREA, OR FOREST

0 10 20 30 40 50 60 70
MILES

N
W E
S

Sawtooth National Forest

Tremonton

Logan
Cache

Wasatch-

Bear Lake

Brigham City

Ogden

National

Forest

Great Salt Lake

Layton

Salt Lake City

West Valley City

Taylorsville

West Jordan

Sandy

Wasatch-Cache National Forest

Tooele

Utah Lake

Orem

Provo

Uinta

Wasatch-Cache National Forest

Heber City

Wasatch-Cache National Forest

Wasatch-Cache National Forest

King's Peak (13,528 ft.)

Weber R.

S. Fk. Duchesne R.

Roosevelt

Vernal

Uinta R.

Duchesne

Strawberry Reservoir
Strawberry R.

Ashley National Forest

Flaming Gorge Reservoir

Ashley National Forest

Green R.

White R.

National

Forest

Nephi

Uinta

National

Forest

Sevier Bridge Reservoir

Ephraim

Fishlake

Sevier R.

Fishlake

National

Forest

Manti-la Sal National Forest

Helper
Price

Price R.

Green R.

Willow Cr.

Sevier Lake (dry)

National

Richfield

Muddy Cr.

Green R.

Arches National Park

Moab

Canyonlands

National

Park

Glen

Forest

Otter Cr.

Dixie

National

Forest

Fremont R.

Capitol Reef National Park

Dirty Devil R.

Cedar City

Dixie

National

Forest

East Fork Sevier R.

Escalante R.

Canyon

Colorado R.

National

Manti-la Sal National Forest

Blanding

Dixie National Forest

Bryce Canyon National Park

Zion National Park

St. George

Sevier R.

Recreation

Lake Powell

Area

San Juan R.

CELEBRATE THE STATES
UTAH

Rebecca Stefoff

BENCHMARK BOOKS

MARSHALL CAVENDISH
NEW YORK

Benchmark Books
Marshall Cavendish Corporation
99 White Plains Road
Tarrytown, New York 10591-9001

Library of Congress Cataloging-in-Publication Data

Stefoff, Rebecca, (date)
Utah / Rebecca Stefoff.
p.   cm. — (Celebrate the states)
Includes bibliographical references and index.
Summary: Discusses the geographic features, history, government, people,
and attractions of the state known as the Beehive State.
ISBN 0-7614-1064-3
1. Utah—Juvenile literature. [1. Utah.] I. Title. II. Series.
F826.3 .S74   2001   979.2—dc21   99-055534

Maps and graphics supplied by Oxford Cartographers, Oxford, England

Photo Research by Candlepants Incorporated

Cover Photo: Photo Researchers Inc. / Art Twomey

The photographs in this book are used by permission and through the courtesy of; *Photo Researchers, Inc.* : Renee Lynn, 6-7; Wysocki Explorer, 10-11; Alan Carey, 24; Renee Lynn, 25(top); Brenda Tharp, 25(bottom); Jerry L. Ferrarra, 26; Jim Steinberg, 34; Bruce M. Herman, 91; N. R. Rowan, 107, 113; Marion Patterson, 114; National Audubon Society Collection, W.V. Cricfi, 117 (top); Jeff Lepore, 120 (top); Alan D. Carey, 120 (bottom); James L. Amos, 135; Margaret Durrance, back cover. *Corbis* : James L. Amos, 14, 64, 79, 86-87,135; David Muench, 17, 22, 23, 60, 110; Scott T. Smith, 18, 29, 68-69, 98-99, 101, 109, 125; Joseph, 54-55; Phil Schermeister, 62, 80, 82; Lynda Richardson, 65; Karl Weatherly, 66; Dean Conger, 67; Richard Cummins, 73; Buddy May, 75; Bettmann, 93, 127 (top), 128, 130, 133; Sergio Carmona, 96; Dewitt Jones, 104, 123; George Lepp, 106; Lynn Goldsmith, 126; Roger Ressmeyer, 127 (bottom); Joyce Nattchayan, 129;Oscar White, 132. *The Image Bank* : Grant U. Faint, 20; Marc Romanelli, 84. *Springville Museum of Art, Springville Utah*: Gift of Lund Wassmer Collection, 30-31; 41. *Jocelyn Art Museum*: 35. *Utah Historical Society, all rights reserved*: photo # 12293, 37; photo # 24341, 40; photo # 00651, 46; photo # 2769, 47; photo # 11915, 49; photo #4215, 51; photo # 00284, 52; photo#13774, 89(right); photo#13589, 131.*Stephen Tremble* : 71. *Salt Lake Convention and Visitor's Bureau* : 76. *Stuart Ruckman* : 81. *Manuscripts Division, J.Willard Marriot Library, University of Utah*: 89(left), 92. *Mrs Fields Original Cookies*: 95. *C/Z Harris* : 117 (bottom).

Printed in Italy

3   5   6   4   2

CONTENTS

UTAH IS . . .

Utah is an awe-inspiring landscape.

"There are deep caverns and rooms resembling ruins of prisons, castles, churches with their guarded walls, battlements, spires, and steeples, niches and recesses, presenting the wildest and most wonderful scene that the eye of man ever beheld; in fact, it is one of the wonders of the world."   —Government surveyor T. C. Bailey describing Bryce Canyon, 1876

"You can never ignore the land here—you can't get away from it. Everywhere you look you see into the real earth, like a skeleton of rock. For a geologist, Utah is just one big paradise."
    —Geologist Karyn De Martinis, on Canyonlands National Park

Utah was founded as a religious colony by the Mormons, who have had a strong influence on the state.

"There is much else about our state's past that is exciting and instructive, but we cannot escape the importance of the Mormon presence or influence here."   —Historian Dean L. May

"It's more than history or religious affiliation, or even this landscape. It's all these: Family. Religion. Place. They can't be divided. . . . By looking to the lake or mountains or into the eyes of a relative, I'm reminded who I am and why I'm here. Could you ask more from a home than that?"   —Terry Tempest Williams, Utah writer and fifth-generation Mormon

Yet Utah is changing, and change may affect the lives of all Utahns.

"It's money lust that's got everybody here working now. The old Mormon culture, the thing that first lifted our community up and held it together for so long, all this new money is killing it."

—Eighty-year-old resident of St. George, 1996

"Hundreds, maybe thousands, of us commute to California. . . . We moved to Utah because it has good schools and an exceptional quality of life—things southern California was offering in lessening amounts. . . . As a newcomer, I consider the state's growth a lot. I know I'm part of what's happening here—both the good and the growing pains. Then I think, hey, this is a terrific place. Maybe in Utah, where society has yet to slip into an unworkable mire, we can take advantage of the clean slate."

—Craig Larson, Salt Lake City, 1996

From snowcapped peaks in the north to red-rock canyons and windswept deserts in the south, Utah is ruggedly beautiful. Native Americans dwelt in this stern, dry, rocky land for thousands of years before waves of newcomers arrived, each seeking something. Mormons wanted a religious homeland, prospectors wanted riches, Hispanic immigrants wanted a chance at a better life. People still come to Utah: mountain bikers searching for thrilling new trails, families looking for happiness in an orderly suburb or a quiet country town. Sometimes called "the land no one wanted," Utah turns out to have exactly what many have sought.

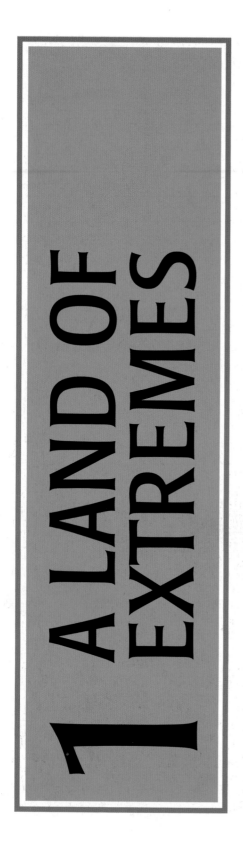

1 A LAND OF EXTREMES

Utah dazzles the eyes and the mind. Sheer pink-and-tan cliffs rear abruptly from fields of yellow and blue wildflowers. Black clouds scud across snow-peaked mountain ranges, trailing drifts of rain like gauzy veils. Far below, the sunbaked desert shimmers in the noonday heat, and tiny, jewel-bright lizards search restlessly for shade. Red-rock towers, carved into a thousand weird shapes by ages of rain and snow, flame scarlet and orange in the setting sun.

Geologist Clarence Dutton felt the magic and majesty of this land. In 1880, after visiting Zion Canyon in southwestern Utah, he wrote of its massive rock walls: "There is an eloquence to their forms which stirs the imagination with a singular power. . . . Nothing can exceed the wondrous beauty of Zion . . . in the nobility and beauty of the sculptures there is no comparison." Many others have felt the same sense of awe. Utah seems much larger than life. The state's mountains are massive and impressive—Paula Huff, author of *Hiking Utah's Summits*, calls Utah "the rooftop of the United States." Utah's gorges and valleys are nearly as deep and every bit as grand as the Grand Canyon, which lies just across the border with Arizona. The state also contains the nation's biggest lake west of the Mississippi River and two of its major rivers.

Utah sits on the western slope of the Rocky Mountains, the backbone of the American West. It is bordered by Colorado on the east, Arizona on the south, Nevada on the west, Idaho on the

LAND AND WATER

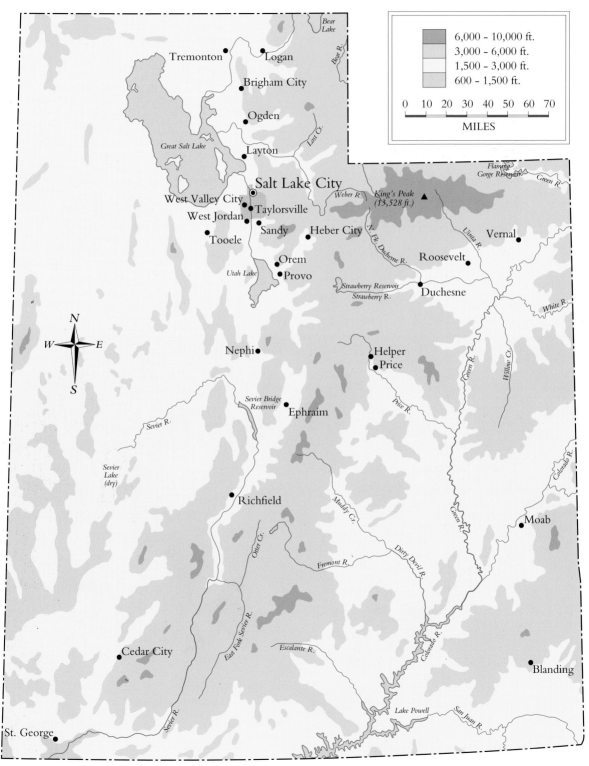

Bear Lake

Tremonton • • Logan

Brigham City •

Ogden •

Bear R.

Lost Cr.

6,000 – 10,000 ft.
3,000 – 6,000 ft.
1,500 – 3,000 ft.
600 – 1,500 ft.

0 10 20 30 40 50 60 70
MILES

Great Salt Lake

Layton •

Flaming Gorge Reservoir

Green R.

Salt Lake City

King's Peak (13,528 ft.) ▲

Weber R.

West Valley City •
West Jordan • • Taylorsville

• Sandy • Heber City

N. Fk. Duchesne R.

Uinta R.

Vernal •

Tooele •

• Orem
• Provo

Roosevelt •

Utah Lake

Strawberry Reservoir
Strawberry R.

Duchesne •

White R.

N
W ✦ E
S

Nephi •

• Helper
• Price

Green R.

Willow Cr.

Sevier Bridge Reservoir

• Ephraim

Price R.

Sevier R.

Sevier Lake (dry)

Colorado R.

Richfield •

Otter Cr.

Muddy Cr.

Green R.

Moab •

Fremont R.

Dirty Devil R.

Cedar City •

East Fork Sevier R.

Escalante R.

Colorado R.

Blanding •

Sevier R.

Lake Powell

San Juan R.

St. George •

north, and Wyoming on the northeast. Utah is divided among three dramatically different geographic regions. They are the Rocky Mountain, Basin and Range, and Colorado Plateau provinces.

THE ROCKY MOUNTAINS

The northeastern corner of Utah, around the notch in the state's square border, is part of the Rocky Mountains. The Wasatch and Uinta mountain ranges meet there at right angles. Between them

The Wasatch Mountains, part of the great Rocky Mountain chain, form northern Utah's backbone.

are green, well-watered valleys. The Cache Valley, a patchwork of tidy farms, orchards, and pastures, is the most fertile part of Utah.

The Green River is the biggest waterway in the region. It flows south from Wyoming into Utah, where it is dammed. The long lake behind the dam is the centerpiece of the Flaming Gorge National Recreation Area, which Utah shares with Wyoming. After passing the dam, the Green River curves briefly into Colorado before it winds and twists its way south into the hilly heart of Utah.

Utah's highest mountains are in the Rocky Mountain province. Many of the Uintas' rounded peaks are more than 12,000 feet high. Utah's highest point, Kings Peak, rises above the rest of the Uintas to a height of 13,528 feet. The Wasatch Mountains stretch south from the Idaho border. The eastern side of the Wasatch Range rises gently from valleys to jagged, snowy summits. On the west, however, the mountain wall is steep and sheer. It forms a rugged line of cliffs and slopes called the Wasatch Front, which drops abruptly from the peaks to the flatland seven thousand feet below. There the Basin and Range province begins.

BASIN AND RANGE

The Basin and Range province, which covers all of western Utah and continues into Nevada, consists of many low, blunt-topped, north-south mountain ranges that one early explorer described as "an army of caterpillars marching to Mexico." The ranges are separated by flat, level valleys called basins.

The Basin and Range province contains some of the least hospitable landscapes in the United States. The old folk song

"Sweet Betsy from Pike," which told of the journey of gold hunters to California in the late 1840s, probably refers to those landscapes: "They came to the desert and salt water lakes/ The ground it was teemin' with varmints and snakes."

This part of Utah certainly has deserts, notably the Great Salt Lake Desert in the northwest, the Sevier Desert in the central west, and the Escalante Desert in the southwest. The Sevier and Escalante Deserts are dry, treeless flatlands similar to many other regions in the West. The Great Salt Lake Desert, however, is unique. Glaringly white and as shiny as glass, it is covered with a thick crust of salt laid down long ago when the sea that once covered the land dried up. Native Americans and early explorers feared crossing this waterless wasteland. Today a favorite pastime of Utahn teenagers is arranging dark rocks to form words and symbols on the white salt borders of the highway that runs through the desert.

Utah also has lakes that have salty water because of minerals in the soil. The most famous of these is the Great Salt Lake. This huge, shallow lake has no outlets. Water that enters the lake stays there, which means that the lake—which averages more than a million acres in area—gets larger or smaller depending upon rainfall and snowmelt. In a wet year, the lake's average depth increases from about thirteen feet to more than thirty-four feet. Its spreading waters cover freeways, farms, and industrial sites and threaten to lap at the streets of the state's capital, Salt Lake City, which perches above the lake's southeastern shore. In a dry year, the lake is shallow and saltier than ever because there is little fresh water to dilute the minerals. At such times the Great Salt Lake reveals its most astounding feature: you can float in it with remarkable ease,

Windblown sagebrush dots the rippling sand dunes of eastern Utah's deserts. Only hardy plants adapted to salty soil and low rainfall can survive here.

because objects, including swimmers, float higher in salt water than in fresh. If you took a dip in the Great Salt Lake when it was low and extra salty, you would find it almost impossible to swim underwater!

Rimmed with salt-crusted rocks, the Great Salt Lake sometimes resembles an arctic sea dotted with gleaming icebergs.

THE COLORADO PLATEAU

Most of eastern and southern Utah—more than half of the state—is part of the Colorado Plateau, which covers the Four Corners region where Colorado, New Mexico, Arizona, and Utah meet. The Colorado Plateau is a broad, rocky highland, but it is not smooth and flat. In some places, layers of rock that lie under the region tilt upward. Their edges are worn away to expose three enormous rows of cliffs, stacked on top of one another. Because each layer is a different color, these are called the Pink, White, and Vermilion (red) Cliffs. Together they create an immense landform called the Grand Staircase of Utah. Elsewhere in the Colorado Plateau are mountains and uncountable ridges, folds, hills, saw-toothed rock reefs, hoodoos (tall spires of rock), mesas (flat-topped, steep-sided uplands), and buttes (similar to mesas but smaller). At 10,388 feet high, Navajo Mountain near the Arizona border is far from the tallest mountain in Utah's Colorado Plateau province, but its broad, cone-shaped outline dominates the horizon for miles around.

These towering features of the landscape are intermingled with gorges, canyons, and valleys that plunge to depths far below the level of the plateau. The Green and Colorado Rivers, which meet in southeastern Utah, carved the widest and deepest of these canyons over millions of years. The Glen Canyon Dam, located just over the Utah border in Arizona, backs the waters of the Colorado up into miles and miles of branching canyons to form Lake Powell, Utah's largest human-made lake.

Fertile valleys nestle among the High Plateau Mountains at the region's western edge and forests carpet some mountaintops and uplands, but much of the Colorado Plateau is desert. The land is worn and windswept rock with only a few pockets of soil here and there to offer a roothold to hardy plants.

PLANTS AND ANIMALS

In the 1950s Edward Abbey worked as a ranger in what is now Arches National Park in eastern Utah. His 1968 book about the experience, *Desert Solitaire: A Season in the Wilderness*, captured the rare beauty of a landscape unknown to most people: "The desert waits outside, desolate and still and strange, unfamiliar and often grotesque in its forms and colors, inhabited by rare, furtive creatures of incredible hardiness and cunning, sparingly colonized by weird mutants from the plant kingdom, most of them as spiny, thorny, stunted and twisted as they are tenacious."

The plants of the desert and canyonland include aromatic sagebrush shrubs and tough mountain juniper trees. (Early settlers wrongly called the mountain junipers cedars, which is why many place names in Utah include the word *cedar*.) Tamarisk, willow, and cottonwood trees grow along the courses of rivers and streams, forming narrow corridors of green across the land. Spruce and fir flourish in the cooler, moister districts. Aspens, whose delicate leaves turn bright gold in the fall, line alpine clearings and meadows. Rarest and most impressive of trees is the bristlecone pine, which grows only in high, windy, open places like clifftops and mountain ledges. Bristlecones are among the longest-lived species on Earth; some trees in Utah are more than three thousand years old. They are not towering forest giants, though—their trunks are gnarled and twisted, and they grow low and close to the ground.

Hiking in Utah's narrow, water-carved "slot canyons" is an adventure that can turn deadly if a sudden thunderstorm produces a flash flood.

This bristlecone pine may have weathered thousands of sunrises and sunsets. A ranger in Bryce Canyon National Park calls bristlecones "the star survivors of the plant world."

For a short time each year, even the most barren parts of Utah blaze forth in a glory of wildflowers. Purple-blue lupine, red Indian paintbrush, and orange globemallow nod in the breeze along country roads. Utah's state flower, the sego lily, carpets meadows with yellow blossoms. Crevices among desert rocks glow with the greenish white flowers of yucca plants, raised high on stiff stalks, and with the white, salmon pink, orange, and red blooms of the prickly pear cactus, delicate petals set amid threatening spikes.

From mountain lakes to desert canyons, Utah's habitats are home to a wide range of animals. Black bears live in the mountains, but they are not really black—in Utah they tend to be golden brown to match the earth tones of the landscape. Rocky Mountain sheep, mountain goats, and mountain lions dwell, as you might expect, in the mountains. So do porcupines, bobcats, martens, and

Stubby beavertail cacti, crowned with pink flowers, contrast with the tall spikes of yucca plants in the Escalante River canyon.

A bear investigates a fisherman's camp. Although bears that live in Utah's forests are dark in color, such as this one, those of the more open canyonlands may be sand- or earth-colored.

beavers. Coyotes live throughout the state. Elk graze in mountain meadows, pronghorn antelope on plateau grasslands, and mule deer along canyon streams. Although some large animals such as mountain lions live in the arid canyonlands, most of the wildlife there is small: mice, snakes, slow-moving tortoises, and lizards. Desert hikers soon learn to check boots and bedrolls for scorpions—flat, fast-moving creatures whose stingers pack a poisonous punch.

The Great Salt Lake, Utah Lake (south of the salt lake), and Bear

A Rocky Mountain bighorn sheep with its young. Prized by hunters, these sturdy animals roam high mountain meadows and crags.

This collared lizard, spotted basking on sandstone in Zion National Park, is one of more than a dozen kinds of lizards found in Utah.

RAPID GROWTH MEETS A SLOW TORTOISE

In the mid-1990s a crisis was brewing in southwestern Utah, around St. George. The town's population had risen from 7,000 in 1970 to 37,500 in 1995, and showed no sign of slowing. Construction of new homes and businesses was chewing up large chunks of once-wild countryside and threatening the well-being—even the survival—of plants and animals in the region.

One of those animals, the Mojave Desert tortoise, became the center of a conflict between those who wanted to preserve the land and those who wanted to develop it. Many tortoises lived right outside St. George, in areas scheduled to be developed. After the government declared the tortoise a threatened species, regulations came into play that could limit construction. Some locals were horrified that a slow-moving, foot-long tortoise that few of them had ever seen might end their town's boom. Meanwhile, environmentalists claimed that some people were trying to get rid of the problem by killing off the tortoises.

While accusations flew, representatives from all sides of the issue struggled to find a compromise. The result was the Red Cliffs Desert Reserve, a sanctuary in Utah's southwestern corner. No one is yet certain whether the tortoise will flourish there. But even some people who were once against protecting the tortoises now appreciate the value of preserving a little bit of Utah untouched. Marshall Topham, who fought to save the tortoises, says, "I hear more and more, 'We don't like tortoises, but at least this prevented parking lots, condos, and golf courses from being everywhere.'"

Lake (straddling the Idaho border) provide habitat for hundreds of thousands of seagulls and other waterbirds. Some of these birds live in Utah year-round, while others rest and feed there during migration. They eat many of the tiny brine shrimp that live in the Great Salt Lake and the brine flies that haunt the lake's shores. Other bodies of water in the state have fish such as trout, catfish, carp, and bass.

SUN, RAIN, AND SNOW

After her first visit to Utah, Oregonian Kathy Carilla offered this advice to anyone planning a similar trip: "Bring extra sunblock!" Sun worshipers love Utah—the state gets more than three hundred sunny days in an average year. Temperatures vary widely, however, and the mountains and high valleys are considerably cooler than the deserts and southern canyons. Utah's highest recorded temperature was 117 degrees Fahrenheit in the southern city of St. George in 1985. Its lowest was –69 degrees at Peter's Sink that same year. Winters are rarely severe except in the high mountains, while summers are long, hot, and dry. Even in the worst hot spells, however, people can cool down by going up the nearest mountain.

Like temperature, precipitation—the total amount of rain and snow—varies dramatically across the state. The driest region, the Great Salt Lake Desert, gets less than 5 inches of precipitation a year. The wettest region, the Wasatch Mountains, receives about 60 inches, enough to provide plenty of snow for skiers at the mountain resorts of Alta and Park City.

In summer, thunderstorms frequently stir the skies over the

Colorado Plateau. Edward Abbey described the skies of August in southern Utah: "By noon the clouds are forming around the horizon and in the afternoon, predictable as sunrise and sunset, they gather in massed formations, colliding in jags of lightning and thunderous artillery, and pile higher and higher toward the summit of the sky in vaporish mountains, dazzling under the sunlight." Often, however, no rain falls from these impressive displays. Or it falls but evaporates in the hot air before reaching the ground. Weather scientists call this phenomenon virga. It is a common sight over the plateau: a veil of rain, dark against the sky, that doesn't touch the earth.

PEOPLE ON THE LAND

The people who settled the West were looking for water, farmland, and timber. In Utah they found these things in the fertile mountain valleys and especially along the Wasatch Front. Today the state's population remains largely concentrated there. Eight of every ten Utahns live in a 120-mile corridor along the front, from Logan in the north through Ogden, Salt Lake City, and Orem, to Provo. Elsewhere in the state are vast stretches of desert and canyonlands with almost no population.

Between these extremes are the small cities and towns such as Cedar City, Vernal, and Nephi that make up the fabric of life outside the Wasatch Front. In these places people have changed the land with their farms, factories, roads, and airports. Dams, irrigation canals, and pumping systems have transformed arid landscapes and changed the shapes of rivers. Mines and mineral-

The town of Logan sits in the shadow of the Wasatch Range. Dramatic contrasts are common in Utah, a patchwork of flatlands and ranges.

extraction plants dot the mountains and basins. Yet parts of Utah still look much as they did when people first arrived there thousands of years ago. You can hike up a ridge or into a canyon, sit on a million-year-old rock, hear nothing but the wind, and see nothing made by human hands between you and the horizon, except perhaps the silver glint of a jet plane creeping across the turquoise sky.

2 "THIS IS THE RIGHT PLACE"

Sunset in Blacksmith Fork Canyon, by Reuben Kirkham

You can see the remains of some of Utah's long-vanished inhabitants at Dinosaur National Monument on the state's eastern border. There scientists search for evidence of the life that stomped through Utah's swamps and swam in its seas a hundred million years ago. This life included the allosaurus, a forty-foot-long meat-eating dinosaur that is the state fossil. Compared with this long history, human life is a recent development. Humans entered Utah between 10,000 and 12,000 years ago. Since then the history of Utah has been about people learning to live in a challenging, sometimes unforgiving, land.

NATIVE AMERICAN CULTURES

The first people in Utah were the Paleo-Indians. They were descended from migrants who entered North America across a land bridge that connected Alaska to Siberia in northeast Asia until about 11,000 years ago. The Paleo-Indians gathered wild plants and hunted birds, rabbits, and other small game. Among the few traces of them that have survived are sharp, beautifully carved spear points.

People in this region learned about farming around 500 B.C. The Anasazi culture emerged in southeastern Utah and elsewhere in the Four Corners area. The Anasazi raised corn, beans, squash, cotton, and turkeys. They created dramatic black-and-white pottery and built complex and sturdy homes of poles, cut stone, and adobe (sun-dried mud brick). After A.D. 1150 they began building large, many-roomed dwellings called pueblos, some perched high on canyon or cliff walls. The center of their civilization, however, lay outside Utah's present borders.

By A.D. 500 the Fremont culture had spread across most of Utah. Fremont people hunted with bows and arrows, grew corn and vegetables, and made clay pottery and statues. They built sturdy stone or adobe buildings called granaries to store food. Many of these granaries still stand, tucked under rock overhangs or into niches in canyons. The Fremont also carved and painted haunting images of animals, geometric shapes, and broad-shouldered, horned human figures on rock walls throughout Utah.

Both the Fremont and Anasazi cultures were waning by 1300. Scientists are not sure why. Perhaps drought had parched their farms, or attacks by other Native American groups weakened them. A few hundred years later, when European explorers arrived, other Native American peoples lived in Utah.

The peaceful Gosiutes inhabited Utah's western deserts and were highly skilled at living in that harsh land. Small bands moved from place to place in search of foods such as deer, small game, pine nuts, berries, and crickets. The Paiutes lived in southern Utah, where they grew crops and developed great skill as basketmakers. Like the Gosiutes, they were peaceful and often suffered attacks from the more aggressive Utes. Daring buffalo hunters and fierce raiders, the Utes sold captive Paiutes and Gosiutes to the Spaniards as slaves. Unlike the other Indians of Utah, who lived in caves, pit

TURNED TO STONE: A PAIUTE TALE

In Bryce Canyon in southern Utah, thousands upon thousands of reddish pink stone towers, often topped with white stone, march in rows for miles along the valley floor. Called hoodoos, they are remnants of rock walls eroded by rain and frost. Utah's Native Americans recognized the strange magic of the canyon. The Paiutes have a story about how the hoodoos came to be:

A long time ago, before there were any Indians, the Legend People lived in Bryce Canyon. There were many kinds of Legend People—birds, animals, and lizards—but they all looked like human beings. And they all painted their faces red and white. But some of the Legend People became bad. They fought among themselves and stole from one another. Instead of making useful things, they destroyed them. Worst of all, they forgot to pay proper respect to the spirits. Their wickedness angered the powerful Coyote. Coyote punished the wicked Legend People by turning them into rocks. You can see them in Bryce Canyon still, all turned to stone. Some are standing in rows, some are sitting down, some are holding onto others. But each is still wearing the color of paint that the Legend People wore on their faces before they became rocks.

Alfred Jacob Miller painted this picture of the Shoshone Indians, who lived in northern Utah.

houses, or brush shelters, the Utes adopted the cone-shaped buffalo-hide tents called tepees from the Great Plains Indians. The Shoshones of northern Utah farmed corn and vegetables, fished, hunted small game, and gathered wild foods. After around 1500 some Navajo moved into southeastern Utah from Arizona and New Mexico. They kept horses and sheep and were master weavers and metalworkers. These were the five tribes that Europeans met when they entered Utah.

EXPLORATION

The European explorers of North America inched their way inland from the coasts. Deep in the center of the continent, Utah was one of the last places in the present United States that they entered.

The first European known to have entered Utah was Juan Antonio Rivera of Santa Fe, New Mexico, an outpost of the Spanish colony in Mexico. In 1765 he led a party of explorers as far north as present-day Moab. Then, in 1776, Francisco Domínguez and Silvestre Vélez de Escalante left Santa Fe in search of a route to the colony of Monterey on the central California coast. They made it all the way to Utah Lake before winter storms sent them back to Santa Fe.

In the years that followed, Spanish and Mexican traders criss-crossed southern Utah, doing business with the Native Americans and traveling between New Mexico and California. When Mexico became independent in 1821, it claimed Utah as part of its northern territory, but in the 1820s outsiders began entering the region. The English came down from Canada, and the Americans came along the Green River. Both sought one of the West's most valuable resources—the sleek, waterproof hide of the beaver, much prized by hatmakers and coatmakers in Europe. Trapping beaver and trading with the Indians for more hides, the mountain men, as they came to be called, nearly made the beaver extinct in the American West. They also explored the region thoroughly and paved the way for those who came later.

Army officer and explorer John C. Frémont, called the Pathfinder, produced reports and maps that inspired many pioneers to head west. His description of the Salt Lake valley made Brigham Young choose Utah as a refuge for the Mormons.

Some of these mountain men became famous. Jim Bridger is believed to have been the first white person to see the Great Salt Lake (he tasted it and thought it was the Pacific Ocean). Kit Carson became a guide for government surveyors and settlers in the region. Jedediah Strong Smith probably knew more about western geography than anyone alive at the time. Smith was the first non-Indian to cross Utah from north to south and from west to east.

By the late 1830s the heyday of the mountain men was past. Around this time the U.S. government began sending army officers such as Benjamin Bonneville and John C. Frémont to explore the region, even parts of it that belonged to Mexico. Frémont made several journeys into Utah in the 1840s. He was fascinated by "that famous lake" of salt water, and he carried out an experiment in which he obtained fourteen pints of "very white salt" from five gallons of Great Salt Lake water. Frémont was the first explorer to realize that no rivers or lakes lead from the Wasatch Front to the Pacific Ocean.

Already a few parties of American settlers had struggled across that desert, bound for California. One pioneer, Heinrich Lienhard, described in his journal the good soil, abundant springs, warm air, and lovely scenery of the Salt Lake valley. He added, "Had there been a single family of white men to be found living here, I believe that I would have remained. Oh, how unfortunate that this beautiful country was uninhabited!" Most of the early travelers were not at all interested in Utah—it was just an obstacle on their way west. But one band of settlers came to stay and has shaped the state to this day.

THE MORMONS

These pioneers were members of the Church of Jesus Christ of Latter-day Saints, sometimes called Mormons or LDS. Their origins lay in New York, where their leader, Joseph Smith, had published a religious text called the Book of Mormon in 1830. Smith's followers added to Christianity the beliefs that Jesus Christ had appeared in America after his death and that an angel had revealed the Book of Mormon to Smith and inspired him to establish a new church.

Smith and the early elders, as adult male Mormons are called, practiced polygamy, or marriage to more than one wife at the same time. They claimed that their religion not only allowed but encouraged plural marriage. Some Americans, however, were outraged by what they viewed as immoral behavior. As a result, the Mormons faced hostility and violence. Because of trouble with non-Mormons, Smith decided that his people should create a new home in the wilderness, outside the United States. In early 1844 he sent elders to examine Oregon and California, to "hunt out a good location where we can . . . build a city in a day, and have a government of our own, get up into the mountains, where the devil cannot dig us out, and live in a healthy climate where we can live as old as we have mind to." Later that year, Smith was killed by an angry mob.

A new leader, Brigham Young, declared that the Mormons would settle near the Great Salt Lake. Soon, Young and about 150 others were making the long journey across the plains on the Mormon Trail, which paralleled the better-known Oregon Trail. Turning south in Wyoming, the pioneers crossed the Uinta Mountains, plodded across a stretch of desert in midsummer heat, and then worked their way up a canyon and through the Wasatch Range. In July 1847 the first of the pioneers came down into the Salt Lake valley. Mormon legend says that Brigham Young took one look around and announced, "This is the right place." In reality, though, Young was ill, riding in the back of a wagon. Some elders reached the site of Salt Lake City, dedicated it as the Mormons' new home, and started plowing. Young's wagon showed up two days later.

Soon thousands of Mormons were traveling the Mormon Trail. Within ten years some 22,000 Mormons lived in Salt Lake City and

Brigham Young organized the migration of the Mormons to Utah. Although Young did not achieve his dream of an all-Mormon homeland, his accomplishments as a leader remain impressive.

other new towns along the Wasatch Front. And new believers kept coming. Today's Mormons look back with special pride on the phase of settlement called the Handcart Migration. Between 1856 and 1860 some three thousand people walked the Mormon Trail without wagons or draft animals. Instead they hauled their possessions westward for a thousand miles in hand-drawn wooden carts. Upon arrival in Mormon territory they found neat homes, wide streets, and a temple under construction in Salt Lake City. They also heard the story of how in 1848 huge swarms of insects had threatened to destroy crops until seagulls from the lake devoured them. The Mormons regarded the gulls as a divine miracle, and the seagull is Utah's state bird today.

The Wasatch Front was not the only area the Mormons settled.

Handcart Pioneer's First View of Salt Lake Valley, *by Carl C. A. Christensen.*

Young sent out groups of new arrivals to establish communities in southern Utah and in neighboring Idaho, Colorado, Nevada, and Arizona. The struggles of these small, isolated settlements, sustained only by faith, were epic. Some failed, but many took root.

TOWARD STATEHOOD

The Mormons had reached their promised land, but they had not yet made it their own. They thought they had left the United States, which a Mormon song of the time called "The blood-stained wicked nation/From whence the Saints have fled." But in 1848 Mexico ceded its northern borderlands, including Utah, to the United States.

Mormon leaders had originally planned to establish an independent Mormon nation in the West. Once the territory fell under American control, they realized that complete independence was not possible, but they still hoped to have a Mormon state. They wanted Congress to create a state called Deseret, from a word used for "honeybee" in the Book of Mormon. Instead Congress created the Utah Territory in 1850. Young was named the territorial governor, but he had to share power with non-Mormon officials sent from Washington, D.C.

Many non-Mormons were fearful and suspicious of Mormon ways. They were concerned not just with polygamy but also with the Mormons' shared ownership of property, their tendency to act as a group rather than as individuals (they formed their own political party and joked that they all voted the same way), and the church's influence on every part of members' lives.

One consequence of this mistrust was the Utah War of 1857. Believing that the Mormons were rebelling against U.S. authority and breaking U.S. laws, President James Buchanan sent soldiers marching toward Utah. The Mormons regarded them as an invading army, and a group of tense and frightened Mormons, together with some local Native Americans, attacked a wagon train of settlers bound for California, killing about 120 people in the Mountain Meadows Massacre. Fortunately, the conflict ended without further disasters, although the government replaced Young as governor of the Utah Territory. Outside Utah, the press printed sensational stories about polygamous marriages and the church's ruthless treatment of those who defied it. Such stories, some untrue, roused popular opinion against the Mormons.

A growing number of non-Mormons were entering Utah. During the 1850s most simply passed through on their way to California, but by the 1860s they were coming to work and stay. Non-Mormon communities sprang up around an army camp established near Salt Lake City in 1862. Around that same time, two events helped open Utah to the outside world. In 1861 the first telegraph line between the Great Plains and California was completed in Salt Lake City. Eight years later an even bigger milestone was reached when two railway lines, one from the west and one from the east, met at Promontory Point in northern Utah to form the first railroad across the United States. The telegraph line carried this message to the world: "The last rail is laid. The last spike is driven. The Pacific railroad is finished."

The discovery of gold and silver in some Utah mountains in the late 1860s brought a flood of prospectors and miners to the territory.

ALL ARE TALKING OF UTAH

In 1868, the two sections of the transcontinental railway were rapidly approaching each other. Their projected meeting point was at Promontory Point, a desolate spot near Ogden, Utah. Many Mormons feared the encroaching hostile world. But Brigham Young, the president of the Mormon Church, said, "I wouldn't give much for a religion which could not withstand the coming of a railroad."

Words attributed to John Davis   **Music By Henry C. Work**

Who'd ev - er think that U - tah would stir the world so much? Who'd ev - er think the Mor - mons were wide - ly known as such? I hard - ly dare to scrib - ble, or such a sub - ject touch, For all are talk - ing of U - tah. Hur - rah! Hur - rah! The Mor - mons have a name. Hur - rah! Hur - rah! They're

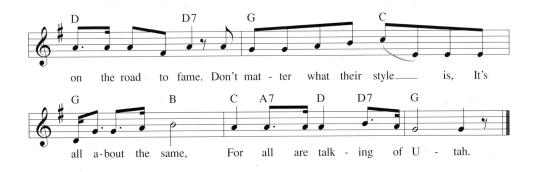

on the road to fame. Don't mat - ter what their style is, It's

all a-bout the same, For all are talk - ing of U - tah.

'Tis Utah and the Mormons in Congress, pulpit, press,
'Tis Utah and the Mormons in every place, I guess.
We must be growing greater, we can't be growing less,
For all are talking of Utah. *Chorus*

They say they'll send an army to set the Mormons right,
Regenerate all Utah, and show us Christian light;
Release our wives and daughters, and put us men to flight,
For all are talking of Utah. *Chorus*

They say that Utah cannot be numbered as a State,
They wished our land divided, but left it rather late.
'Tis hard to tell of Mormons, what yet may be their fate,
For all are talking of Utah. *Chorus*

Whatever may be coming, we cannot well forsee,
For it may be the railroad, or some great prodigy.
At least the noted Mormons are watching what's to be,
For all are talking of Utah. *Chorus*

I now will tell you something you never thought of yet,
We bees are nearly filling the "Hive of Deseret."
If hurt we'll string together, and gather all we get,
For all are talking Utah. *Chorus*

In the rush to build the first railroad across the United States, two railway companies raced toward each other from west and east. In 1869 they met on the northern shore of the Great Salt Lake, at a place now called the Golden Spike National Historic Site.

They built towns of crude wooden buildings high on mountain slopes. To serve them came merchants and traders, many of whom set up shop in Salt Lake City. The non-Mormon population of Utah grew from about 8 percent in 1860 to 34 percent in 1890—a trend

Early gold miners in Utah. As at other gold-rush sites in the West, very few individual prospectors became rich. Most wealth from mining went to corporations, although hardy individuals still stake and work small claims in Utah's mountains.

that pleased U.S. officials who wanted to "Americanize" the Mormon territory.

As early as 1850 the influx of newcomers to Utah had caused problems for Native Americans, who had no desire to give up their hunting and gathering grounds. During the 1850s and 1860s Indians threatened white settlements, attacked stagecoach stations, and killed a government survey team. In 1863 U.S. troops in Utah ended the Shoshone resistance, killing some 250 of them in the Battle of Bear River. The following year Congress ordered the Utes to move to the Uintah Reservation. After a short but bitter war they reluctantly did so. The Navajo of southern Utah were forced onto their own reservation in 1884.

Congress firmly refused to consider statehood for Utah until the Mormons gave up polygamy. Congress also passed laws against polygamy that sent hundreds of Mormons to jail and others into hiding. Realizing that Congress would not soften its stand, in 1890 Wilford Woodruff, the president of the church, advised all members "to refrain from contracting any marriage forbidden by the law of the land." The Mormons also disbanded their political party. Seeing that Utah was moving closer to the mainstream of America, Congress made it the forty-fifth state in 1896.

THE TWENTIETH CENTURY

Once Utah became a state, its history was linked to that of the United States as a whole. The trends and events that shaped its development were the same ones that swept across the rest of America—the growth of cities, for example. As America slowly

BADLANDS AND OUTLAWS

During the late nineteenth and early twentieth centuries the wild terrain of the Colorado Plateau offered hiding places to a number of colorful outlaws. The most famous was Robert LeRoy Parker, who used the name Butch Cassidy. Born in Beaver, Utah, he started out as a cowboy, moved on to cattle stealing, and then became a bank and train robber. During most of the 1890s he led a criminal gang called the Wild Bunch that terrorized the West from Montana to Nevada. Between raids they holed up in hideouts such as Robbers' Roost in Utah. Detectives and marshals were closing in on the gang when Cassidy and his partner, Harry Longabaugh, known as the Sundance Kid, fled to South America in 1901. They became outlaws there, too, and are believed to have died in a shootout with authorities in 1909. But rumors have always shrouded their final moments. Robert Parker's sister later claimed that her brother secretly returned to the United States in 1925 and lived quietly in the Pacific Northwest until his death in 1937.

shifted from a land of farms to a land of factories, industry replaced agriculture as the state's main source of jobs. By the 1920s less than a third of Utahns were farmers.

During the early decades of statehood, Utah's chief industry was mining—not just gold and silver, but copper and coal as well. Many people worked in factories related to the mining industry, such as ore smelters and metalworking plants. The rise of industry brought its own problems, however. Workers received low wages for long, exhausting work in often dangerous conditions. After an explosion in a coal mine at Scofield killed two hundred men in 1900, mine workers in Utah began demanding changes. They tried to form unions that could negotiate for better wages and working conditions but faced stiff opposition from owners and managers who wanted to keep operating costs down. In 1915 the attention of laborers around the world focused on Utah when Joe Hill, a Swedish immigrant who was a member of the Industrial Workers of the World union, was arrested for shooting two people during a robbery attempt. Although the poems and songs Hill wrote while in prison awaiting trial won him sympathy, he was found guilty and executed. The evidence suggests that Hill did commit the crime, but many observers felt that his trial was conducted unfairly because he was a foreigner and a labor-union member.

While World War I raged overseas from 1914 to 1918, demand for Utah's farm and factory products kept the state's economy

At smelters such as this one in Park City in the early twentieth century, rock from the mines was crushed and melted to extract its metallic ores.

humming. After the war, however, the economy slumped. The slump got worse in 1929, when a severe economic depression gripped the nation. The Great Depression struck especially hard at Utah, which had one of the country's highest unemployment rates. A third of Utahn workers were jobless. Not until the United States entered World War II in 1941 did the state's economy fully

Tooele Army Depot west of Salt Lake City was one of several military installations built in Utah during World War II. At war's end in 1945, more than one-quarter of all civilian income in the state came from government jobs, most of them in the defense industry.

recover. Utah's vast empty lands were perfect for new military installations, such as air bases and the Dugway Proving Ground near the Great Salt Lake Desert where weapons were tested.

Later in the century Utah's economy shifted again, this time to include the tourism and recreation industries as well as high-technology industries. As the twentieth century ended Utah was busy with preparations for the 2002 winter Olympics, to be held in and around Salt Lake City.

At the dawn of the twenty-first century Utahns face challenges familiar to many Americans: economic development, environmental protection, urban renewal, raising funds for education and the arts. They also face the challenge of finding common ground and shared values, whatever their religious beliefs. Mormons and non-Mormons alike hope that the state's heritage will equip it to meet the future. "I disagree with plenty of things about the LDS," says a non-Mormon woman who moved to Utah from Colorado. "But I like their optimism and their energy. They have a tradition of sharing, caring for one another, and working cooperatively. I hope that all of us here can learn something from that as we enter the next millennium."

3 MAKING IT WORK

The capitol in Salt Lake City

Utah's Mormon founders dreamed of a society whose government and economy would be shaped by the church. Today, however, Utah's state government operates like those of the other forty-nine states, and its economy is intertwined with that of the rest of the nation and the world.

INSIDE GOVERNMENT

The government of Utah, like the federal government, consists of three branches—executive, legislative, and judicial—that perform different functions.

Executive. The executive branch is responsible for putting the state's laws and policies into action. It is headed by the governor, who is elected to a four-year term. Other executive officials are the lieutenant governor, who takes over if the governor cannot fulfill his or her duties, and the state's attorney general, treasurer, and auditor. Various departments and agencies oversee a host of government services such as education, tax collection, environmental protection, and road maintenance. Some officials who administer these services are elected, while the governor appoints others.

Legislative. The legislative branch makes the state laws. It consists of a senate and a house of representatives. The twenty-nine senators serve four-year terms; the seventy-five representatives serve

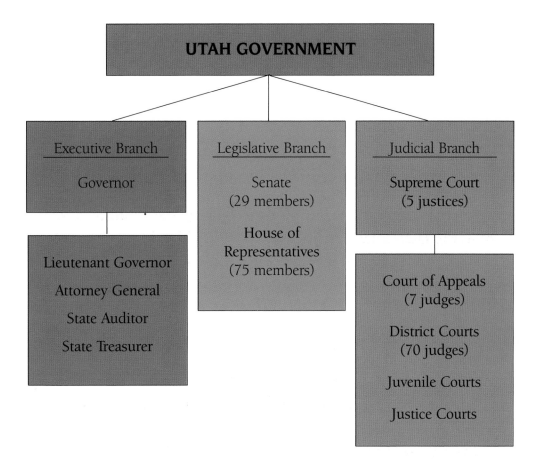

two-year terms. They develop bills that propose new laws or change existing laws and then vote on whether to make the bills into laws. If both houses pass a bill it goes to the governor, who can either sign it into law or turn it down by vetoing it. A bill vetoed by the governor can still become law if two-thirds of the legislature votes for it.

Judicial. The judicial branch is responsible for hearing legal cases and interpreting state law. There are three sets of trial courts: district courts for serious cases; justice courts where justices of the peace hear minor cases; and juvenile courts for cases involving young people. Someone not satisfied with the verdict of one of these lower courts can ask the court of appeals to hear the case. The court of appeals consists of seven judges who serve six-year terms. Appeals from this court go to Utah's five-member supreme court, which also rules on whether or not laws conform to the state's constitution. The governor appoints the supreme court justices to ten-year terms, but they must be approved by the voters in the next election.

MAKING A MARK

Although Utah was one of the last states to enter the Union, it has achieved several notable landmarks. Utah was the second state to allow women to vote (Wyoming was the first). In 1896 Utahns became the first Americans to elect a woman to their state senate. As a legislator, Martha Hughes Cannon worked to create a state board of health. Nearly a century later, in 1985, Jake Garn, a U.S. senator from Utah, became the first federal legislator to travel in space during his term of office when he orbited Earth 109 times in the space shuttle *Discovery*.

FIGHTING FOR THE LAND

The hottest political issues in modern Utah revolve around the land—whose is it, and how shall it be used? Like other western states, Utah includes a great deal of land owned and managed by federal agencies such as the Bureau of Land Management and the U.S. Forest Service. More than 65 percent of Utah is federal land—

a higher percentage than in any other state except Alaska. Utah has taken a leading role in what some call the "sagebrush rebellion," efforts by western states to gain greater control over the use of federal land and resources.

Some of the most heated debates in Utah's recent history revolved around the creation of Grand Staircase–Escalante National Monument in 1996. Some Utahns are strongly opposed to monument status for this Delaware-sized piece of desert. Although the Bureau of Land Management still administers the land—as it did before—the region's status as a national monument means more restrictions. For instance, a Dutch corporation had to halt plans for large-scale coal mining in the monument, enraging Utahns who expected the mining operation to be a source of income. Senator Orrin Hatch of Utah called the monument a federal land grab, even though the land belonged to the federal government, not to the state, before it

GROSS STATE PRODUCT: $61 BILLION

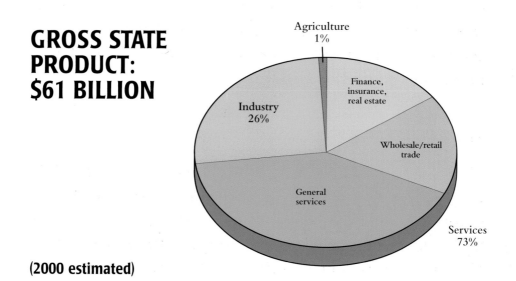

Agriculture
1%

Finance, insurance, real estate

Industry
26%

Wholesale/retail trade

General services

Services
73%

(2000 estimated)

was made into a monument. A local politician compared the establishment of the monument to the "invasion" of 1857, despite the fact that grazing and hunting can continue within the monument.

But Ross Anderson, a Salt Lake City politician, argues that many Utahns want to see their land protected. "The view that all Utahns are up in arms because of the designation of this national monument is a horrible misconception," he says. "Most people love this state because of the incredible beauty."

A CHANGING ECONOMY

The Mormons adopted the beehive as their symbol because bees are industrious and work together for the common good. Utah is still a hardworking place, with an unemployment rate of less than 4 percent (below the national average) in the late 1990s. Yet its economy has changed greatly from the days of Brigham Young, who envisioned an agricultural paradise.

Fewer than 2 percent of Utahns now work in agriculture, although farms and ranches still contribute to the state economy. Beef, sheep, hay, barley, corn, sugar beets, potatoes, and fruits such as apples and cherries are the major agricultural products.

Many more Utahns are employed in service industries such as law and health care. The service sector also includes tourism, one of the fastest-growing parts of Utah's economy, which brings in $3.3 billion

Sandstone pinnacles tower in one-thousand-foot-deep Escalante Canyon, part of the controversial Grand Staircase–Escalante National Monument in the southern part of the state.

A beehive sculpture tops a building on the campus of Brigham Young University in Provo. The beehive, which represented hard work and unity to the Mormons, has become Utah's state symbol.

a year. Tourism has transformed some parts of rural Utah. On any weekend as many as 10,000 rafters, hikers, and mountain bikers converge on the tiny town of Moab, which has greeted the tourist boom with coffee shops, inns, trendy restaurants, outfitters who supply gear to the adventurous, and boutiques where anyone can buy stylish sportswear that at least looks adventurous. "This was a dying uranium town," says a Moab bartender, recalling the days before the

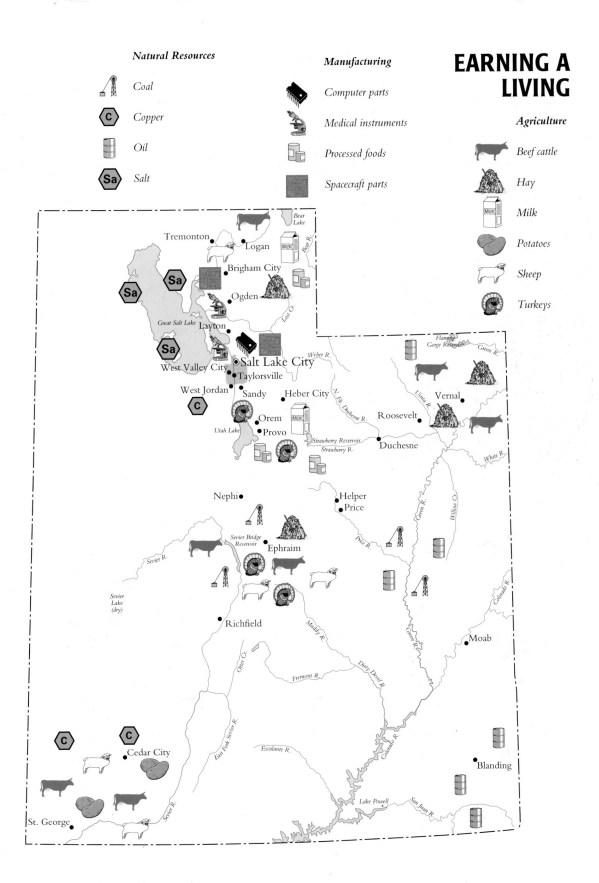

EARNING A LIVING

Natural Resources

Coal
C Copper
Oil
Sa Salt

Manufacturing

Computer parts
Medical instruments
Processed foods
Spacecraft parts

Agriculture

Beef cattle
Hay
Milk
Potatoes
Sheep
Turkeys

Bear Lake
Tremonton
Logan
Brigham City
Ogden
Great Salt Lake
Layton
West Valley City
Salt Lake City
Taylorsville
West Jordan
Sandy
Heber City
Utah Lake
Orem
Provo
Bear R.
Lost Ck.
Weber R.
N. Fk. Duchesne R.
Strawberry Reservoir
Strawberry R.
Flaming Gorge Reservoir
Green R.
Uinta R.
Vernal
Roosevelt
Duchesne
White R.
Nephi
Helper
Price
Sevier Bridge Reservoir
Ephraim
Price R.
Green R.
Willow Ck.
Colorado R.
Sevier R.
Sevier Lake (dry)
Richfield
Muddy R.
Moab
Otter Ck.
Fremont R.
Dirty Devil R.
Colorado R.
East Fork Sevier R.
Escalante R.
Cedar City
Sevier R.
Lake Powell
San Juan R.
Blanding
St. George

Although farming and ranching now employ few Utahns, some families still proudly run operations such as this sheep ranch.

BEEHIVE STATE HONEY CARROT CAKE

Honey is one of the many tastes of Utah, and Utahn beekeepers claim that the best honey is made from their state's spring wildflowers. You can enjoy it in this quick, easy, and nutritious cake. Have an adult help you with this recipe.

½ cup honey
1 egg
⅓ cup canola oil
1 teaspoon cinnamon
1 teaspoon salt
1 teaspoon vanilla
2 4½ ounce jars strained carrot baby food (it's a lot easier than grating carrots by hand!)
1½ cups flour
1 teaspoon baking powder
½ teaspoon baking soda
½ cup golden raisins, chopped nuts, or crushed pineapple (optional)

Start by preheating your oven to 350 degrees. You will need an 8-inch by 8-inch baking pan with a nonstick surface, or put waxed paper in the bottom of the pan.

Mix together the honey, egg, canola oil, cinnamon, salt, and vanilla. Then add the carrots. Next, blend in the flour, baking powder, and baking soda. For a chewier cake add the raisins, nuts, or pineapple—or all three.

Pour the batter into the pan and bake it for 40 to 45 minutes. Test to see if the cake is done by sticking a toothpick into the center. If the toothpick comes out clean, the cake is ready to come out of the oven. Let it cool, and then enjoy it, plain or topped with powdered sugar, frosting—or a drizzle of Utah honey.

"It's the ultimate ride!" exclaimed one mountain biker after an exhilarating adventure on the Moab Slickrock Trail. Here the trail crosses a stretch of smooth, polished sandstone.

boom. And Park City and Alta were mountain backwaters before skiing became big business.

Trade is also important to the Utah economy, as are government jobs—the state government is Utah's largest employer. Other Utahns work in manufacturing or mining. Mining gold and silver in Utah peaked in the late nineteenth century, and other operations have declined since the 1970s, although the state still produces some coal, copper, natural gas, and oil. But as traditional industries slumped, new ones rose to take their place. Since the 1970s a number of companies that design and manufacture computer and communications products have established themselves in Utah. Meanwhile, population growth, especially along the Wasatch Front, keeps transportation and construction workers busy.

In 1999 Governor Mike Leavitt said, summing up Utah's present and its future, "Nothing is as certain in this state as growth. . . . This is a moment in time to shape this generation's obligation and opportunity. How will it be used? Will we continue to grow without plan or purpose, or will our growth be guided by wisdom and logic?" Utahns will create their answers to those questions as the state moves forward in the twenty-first century.

A surveyor takes measurements for a new stretch of highway. The end of the twentieth century saw a flurry of highway construction and other building around Salt Lake City as Utah prepared to host the coming winter Olympics.

4 LIFE IN THE BEEHIVE STATE

"Who wouldn't want to live here?" asks JoElle Welbauer, who moved from Illinois to Salt Lake City with her family in 1994. "We've got good weather, safe streets, friendly neighbors, good jobs, and the great outdoors at our doorstep—even though we hardly ever get out of the valley, we're so busy. It took me a while to get used to the fact that Salt Lake isn't really a metropolis like Chicago, but the small-town values here really make me feel that this is a good place to bring up our kids."

A lot of people agree with the Welbauers, it seems. Utah's population was the fourth fastest-growing in the country between 1990 and 1998. "The word has gotten out that Utah offers the good life," remarks a retired schoolteacher who has lived in Provo for all of her sixty-four years. "Now let's hope we can keep it that way."

THE MORMON HERITAGE

Utah is home to people of many different religions. It has a Roman Catholic cathedral, Protestant churches, Jewish synagogues, and Zen Buddhist meditation centers. Still, the state remains overwhelmingly Mormon. Seven of every ten Utahns are LDS. The Mormon dominance is not likely to change soon, even though the state's population is growing fast. A recent study announced,

Religious ceremonies such as this sacrament meeting are a key part of family and community life for Mormons.

"Utah, the promised land to which Brigham Young brought the Mormon pioneers, is getting more Mormon, not less."

There are two reasons for the steady growth of the Mormon Church in Utah. One is that Mormons favor large families, which means that lots of babies are born into the church. This explains why Utah's average household size is the largest of any state in the nation and why it has the youngest population and the second-highest birth rate. In addition, many Mormons relocate to Utah—the heartland of their faith—from elsewhere. Nearly two-thirds of the people who move to Utah are LDS. Some of them joined the church as the result of the efforts of Mormon missionaries. The church maintains one of the most active missionary programs in the world today. Young men are expected to spend two years spreading the word about their faith in the United States and abroad, and young unmarried women may do the same.

The qualities that the church encourages in its members contribute to the quality of life in Utah. In general, Mormons are sober, modest, optimistic, hardworking, and family-oriented, with a strong commitment to helping each other. Because they have a reputation for sticking together in business and social life, however, some non-Mormons can feel shut out by the state's Mormon majority. As Utah historian Dean L. May writes, "Here both Mormons and non-Mormons are prone to quickly stereotyping others after determining the all-important question, 'Are they or aren't they (Mormon)?'"

Some of those stereotypes concern marriage. Mormons are supposed to marry not just for life but "for eternity." They believe that non-Mormons regard marriage and divorce too casually. Some Mormons in Utah and elsewhere in the West still practice polygamy. The church has maintained its official position against polygamy and casts out members who openly enter into plural marriages, but those who follow the custom without the church's blessing still consider themselves true Mormons.

Still, many non-Mormons share the views of Dale Boucette, a resident in Salt Lake City, who says, "Mormons make good neigh-

A traditional Mormon wedding is reenacted at This Is the Place State Park.

bors and good citizens, and I really don't care what they believe or what they do behind closed doors."

ETHNIC UTAH

Utah's first settlers were all of one faith, and almost all were white and of northern European descent. Religious, racial, and ethnic

ETHNIC UTAH

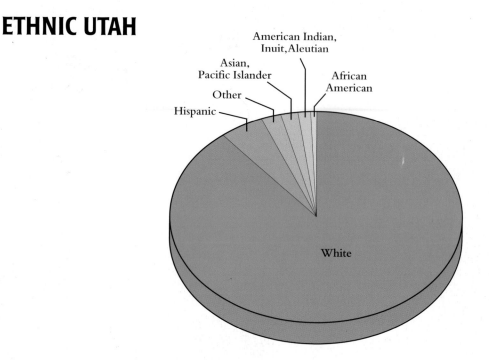

American Indian,
Inuit, Aleutian

Asian,
Pacific Islander

African
American

Other

Hispanic

White

diversity have increased a bit since then, but the state is still 70 percent Mormon and 94 percent white.

Native Americans today make up only 1.4 percent of the state's population. Some of them live on the large Uintah and Ouray Indian Reservation in the east or the Navajo Reservation in the south. There are also two smaller reservations in western Utah. Indians are not Utah's smallest minority, however—fewer than 1 percent of Utahns are African Americans. One reason the black community has remained small is that the Mormon faith has not attracted many black believers. The rest of Utah's population consists of 2 percent Asians and Pacific Islanders, many of whom are LDS, and 5 percent people of Hispanic origin, the state's fastest-growing minority.

Non-Mormons did not arrive in significant numbers in Utah until

A Navajo girl is surrounded by the majestic buttes of Monument Valley, part of the Navajo Reservation in southeastern Utah. The reservation, one of the nation's largest, stretches into New Mexico and Arizona.

the 1860s. The first came to build railroads and work in mines and ore smelters. American companies advertised for workers in foreign cities. Often these workers arrived in the United States unable to speak any English, carrying only a piece of paper with "Salt Lake City" printed on it as a guide to their destination.

The first to arrive were the Chinese in the 1860s and 1870s. By the 1890s most of them had moved to neighborhoods in Salt Lake City

Salt Lake City's annual Days of '47 parade has room for entertainment of all sorts.

POPULATION GROWTH: 1860–2000

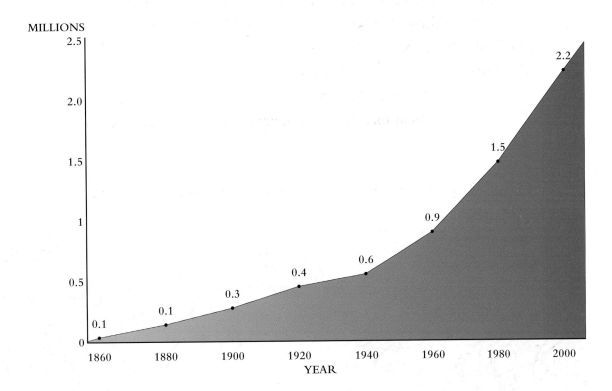

(where New Year's parades traditionally featured a two-hundred-foot-long Chinese dragon), Ogden, and Park City. In the 1880s Japanese workers began moving to Utah. After 1890 the Hashimoto family of Salt Lake City became a leading supplier of labor to western railroads and industries. Although the Japanese came originally as laborers, many of them stayed on as farmers, growing celery and strawberries in Salt Lake, Weber, and Box Elder Counties.

Immigrants from Italy began arriving in the 1870s. Some of the early Italian immigrants converted to Mormonism and became rural farmers. But most worked in mines in Bingham, Stockton, and

Mercur, where Catholic churches were built and Italian-American neighborhoods developed. Today, these "Little Italy" communities have faded away as the descendants of the immigrants have blended with the larger population. The next wave of immigrants were eastern Europeans, followed by Greeks. By 1910 Greeks were the largest immigrant group in Utah. Greek Americans maintained their cultural identity, partly through participation in their national religion. The first Greek Orthodox church in Utah was built in Salt Lake City in 1905. This and other Greek Orthodox churches became focuses of ethnic identity as well as religious worship.

Wherever they came from, immigrants followed the same pattern. Men arrived first, expecting to work for a few years and then return to their homelands. But some decided to stay and sent for wives and families to join them. Each group tended to cluster together in tight communities, where, as one Italian American recalled, they "kept aspects of life with which they were most familiar. Language, customs, basic religious beliefs, family life, and food were important." Most immigrants were laborers, but their children and grandchildren often became shopkeepers, business owners, and farmers.

Each immigrant group, however small, sought to find the right balance between maintaining its identity and blending into larger Utah. Today's Asian, Pacific, and Hispanic immigrants are seeking the same balance. Martin Indurreal first came to Utah as a seasonal fruit picker and now lives with his family near Cedar City. He says, "I will always be Mexican—that is not something you can escape, even if I wanted to. But I wanted the schools here and the life here for my children, and this is my home now."

FAIRS AND FESTIVALS

Each season brings a full slate of fairs and festivals to Utah.

Salt Lake City buzzes with events all summer long. May brings the Living Traditions Festival, a celebration of ethnic culture and folk arts. During the last week of June the Utah Arts Festival turns downtown into a stage for art exhibits and outdoor performances. July 1 launches what one newspaper writer calls "the granddaddy of all our fairs," the Days of '47 celebration, featuring an extremely challenging rodeo and an art show. About half a million people a year attend the celebration, which ends with one of the country's largest parades on July 24, the anniversary of the date Brigham Young reached the valley. In September comes the ten-day state fair, which offers something for just about everyone, with another rodeo, rides and games, animal shows and auctions, and big-name entertainers.

Other festivals around the state include Wheat and Beet Days in Tremonton, the Sundance Film Festival, hosted by actor Robert Redford in Park City in January, Greek Days each July in Price, the Paiute Pow Wow in Cedar City in June, a Mountain Man Rendezvous twice a year in Fort Buenaventura State Park, and reenactments of the ceremony at Promontory Point in which the last spike—a golden one—was driven to complete the transcontinental railroad. "If you can't find something to do here," says a fifteen-year-old boy from Brigham City, "you're not looking."

EDUCATION AND THE ARTS

Utahns are proud of their state's educational achievements, which are linked to the Mormons' belief in the importance of learning. Brigham Young said, "Education is the power to think clearly, to act well in the day's work, and to appreciate life." About 94 percent of adult Utahns can read and write, giving the state one of

Brigham Young University students rest and read beneath a sculpture called The Tree of Life. *The Mormon Church has traditionally placed a high value on education and reading.*

Educators in an increasingly diverse Utah hope that smaller classes will benefit all students.

the highest literacy rates in the nation, and a recent study revealed that Utah also has one of the highest rates of computer literacy. The state ranks sixth in the nation in the percentage of adults who have graduated from high school.

Yet Utah's schools are not without problems. In 1998 Utahn members of the National Education Association (NEA) called attention to large class size in many of the state's schools. The steady

growth of Utah's population, they argued, had not been matched by a rise in funding for teachers and schools. Education activists launched a program that, with the support of the state's lawmakers, may reduce the size of classes in middle schools so that each teacher can concentrate on fewer children—a program that has already been enacted in Utah's elementary schools.

"Our ambassador to the world" is how one Utahn described her state's famed Mormon Tabernacle Choir.

Utah is home to many noted arts institutions, including the Utah Symphony, Ballet West, and the Utah Opera Company. But none of these is more famous than the Mormon Tabernacle Choir, which since 1867 has sung in a special building that the Mormons constructed for musical worship. The choir has made many records and has broadcast radio concerts since 1929. One historian regards

The canyonlands near Moab offer serene, uncluttered camping—with extraordinary views thrown in.

the choir, in which several hundred people "express themselves as a unified, harmonious whole," as the perfect symbol of Mormon culture.

OUT AND ABOUT

Utah boasts only one major-league sports team, but it's a great one. The Utah Jazz of the National Basketball Association, led by star players Karl Malone and John Stockton, brought home many victories during the 1990s.

For the many Utahns young and old who prefer to play sports rather than watch them, the state offers a multitude of playgrounds, parks, ski slopes, forests, and lakes, and plenty of plain old empty space. "What's the big news in sports in Utah right now? The Olympics!" a ski instructor at Park City exclaimed in 1999. "Everyone I know wants to go to some of the events. It's going to be awesome! And I predict we're going to see a lot more kids skiing and skating here afterward."

But some Utahns claim that the best recreation in their state won't be featured in the 2002 Olympics. "Camping, pure and simple," declares thirteen-year-old Heather Perkins. "It doesn't matter if you want lakes, mountains, deserts, forests—we have it all."

5 UNIQUE UTAHNS

Utah is famous for more than its extraordinary landscape, its dramatic history, and its upbeat economy. Some notable folks have come out of—and been drawn to—the Beehive State.

LITERATURE

Utah has nurtured great writers, many of whom drew their inspiration from the land and its people. One who gained considerable fame was historian and literary critic Bernard de Voto. Born in 1897 in Ogden, de Voto had a frontier childhood. "By the time we were eight we went on day-long explorations of the foothills, miles from home," he recalled. By the time he was fourteen he and his friends were camping for weeks at a time "with or without a tent," a hundred miles from home. After graduating from Harvard University in Massachusetts in 1920, de Voto returned to Utah for a time before settling in Massachusetts. Part of his heart, however, always remained in the West, the subject of much of his writing. His most important book, for which he won the Pulitzer Prize in history, is *Across the Wide Missouri*, an account of the pioneer experience.

Although she later traveled the world, Virginia Sorensen was also a child of Utah, born into a Danish-American pioneer family in Provo in 1912. She drew on family and community history for such works as *The Evening and the Morning*, which is set in Utah. In

Bernard de Voto helped
introduce American
readers to their pioneer
heritage.

Although Virginia
Sorensen saw much
of the world, she set
several of her best-
loved books in her
home state of Utah.

1953 she began writing children's books. The best known are *Plain Girl* and *Miracles on Maple Hill*, both about Pennsylvania families, but the most fascinating to anyone interested in Utah is *The House Next Door*, the story of a teenage girl trying to adjust to life in Salt Lake City at the dawn of the twentieth century.

Like Sorensen, John Dennis Fitzgerald was born in Utah and wrote books for both adults and children. He drew on memories of his early life for such books as *Papa Married a Mormon*, but many young readers remember him best for the seven books in his Great Brain series, which he began in the late 1960s. Based on his own childhood and his relationship with his brother, the Great Brain books chronicle the wacky schemes and misadventures of two brothers growing up in Utah.

A major trend in American literature since the 1970s has been authors who write about the West. Wallace Stegner helped start that trend. Born in Iowa, Stegner spent much of his childhood in Utah. He graduated from the University of Utah in 1930 and later taught there before moving on to teach creative writing at Harvard and at Stanford University in California, where he founded a well-known writing program. Stegner wrote more than two dozen fiction and nonfiction books about the West. Among the best known are *Mormon Country*, a collection of anecdotes about and impressions of Utah and the Mormons; *The Big Rock Candy Mountain*, a family saga about homesteading on the Great Plains; and *The Gathering of Zion*, an account of the migration along the Mormon Trail. *Angle of Repose*, a novel about a historian whose efforts to write about his pioneer grandparents lead to greater understanding of his own life, won the Pulitzer Prize in fiction. Stegner was passionate about

WALLACE STEGNER'S COUNTRY

Published in 1941, *Mormon Country* introduced many Americans to a land, a history, and a culture that few had yet explored. Wallace Stegner captured readers' imaginations with vivid descriptions like this haunting account of Utah's landscapes:

It is not merely the immensity and the loneliness and the emptiness of the land that bothers a man caught alone in it. The feeling is not the same that one gets on the great plains, where the sky is a bowl and the earth a disc and the eye is invited to notice the small things because the large ones are so characterless. In the Plateau Country the eye is not merely invited but compelled to notice the large things. From any point of vantage the view is likely to be open not with the twelve- or fifteen-mile radius of the plains but with a radius that is often fifty and sometimes even seventy-five miles—and that is a long way to look, especially if there is nothing human in sight. The villages are hidden in the canyons and under the cliffs; there is nothing visible but the torn and slashed and windworn beauty of absolute wasteland. And the beauty is death. Where the grass and trees and bushes are stripped off and the world laid naked you can see the globe being torn down and rebuilt.

In many of his books, Wallace Stegner urged careful stewardship of America's western lands. One of the themes of his work is that although the West is rugged, it is also fragile and needs our respect and protection.

environmental protection and other causes such as artistic freedom. In 1992 he refused to accept the National Medal for the Arts from the president in protest against what he called "political controls" on the grants given to artists by National Endowment for the Arts.

SCIENCE AND BUSINESS

You may not know it, but you have a Utahn to thank every time you turn on your television. Philo T. Farnsworth came up with the idea for television when he was still a farm boy who rode a horse to school.

Farnsworth was a Utahn through and through—his grandfather founded the town of Beaver, where Farnsworth was born in 1906, at Brigham Young's request. Young Farnsworth was fascinated with science, especially electricity, and he taught himself as much about it as he could, receiving encouragement and inspiration from a chemistry teacher at his high school in Rigby, Idaho. At age fourteen, while plowing a potato field, Farnsworth realized that a beam of electrons could scan a picture and transmit it through the air. He

Inventor Philo Farnsworth in 1928, with the transmitting device of his television set. Sadly, his relationship with his invention later soured.

built the first working model when he was twenty-one. When its camera sent a picture to a receiver in the next room, Farnsworth calmly said, "There you are, electronic television."

If you think that fame and fortune were heaped on the inventor of television, you're wrong. Another engineer had applied for a patent on a similar device. He had not made a working model, but he was connected with the powerful Radio Corporation of America (RCA). Farnsworth launched a long legal battle in an attempt to prove that RCA owed him royalties on the televisions it made. Finally, in 1934, the patent office determined that Farnsworth was the inventor, but it was years before he collected any royalties. In the end RCA managed to take control of the manufacture of televisions without paying the inventor much. In his later years Farnsworth was bitter about the way his invention was being used. His son recalled, "I suppose you could say that he felt he had created a monster, a way for people to waste a lot of their lives."

But if you want to waste a lot of your life sprawled on your couch watching television, why not enjoy fresh, delicious cookies while you channel-surf? Debbi Fields hopes that you do. After people raved about her chocolate-chip cookies, she and her husband, Randy, opened a cookie store in 1977. Other stores followed. The business was originally based in California, but on a skiing trip to Park City they drove their car into a snowbank. A kindly stranger happened along, towed the car out, and wouldn't let them pay him for his trouble. ("Of course he wouldn't! People just help each other out," explains a Salt Lake City bookstore clerk.) The Fieldses were so impressed that in 1981 they moved to Park City and made it their headquarters. By 1988 the company was selling more than $100

Debbi Fields and her husband turned her recipe for chocolate-chip cookies into a recipe for success.

million worth of cookies a year—a lot of dough no matter how you look at it. Salt Lake City is now the headquarters of Mrs. Fields Original Cookies.

A SPORTS HERO

He spent the most glorious years of his career in San Francisco, not Utah, but Steve Young's roots stretch back to the birth of the Beehive State, and Utahns are proud to call him their own.

Steve Young, shown here in 1991, led the San Francisco 49ers of the National Football League to many victories—and made Utahns proud.

Quarterback Steve Young, one of the all-time top football players, is a great-great-great grandson of Brigham Young. He was born in Salt Lake City in 1961. His family later moved to Connecticut, but when the time came for Steve to go to college, he returned to Utah to attend Brigham Young University, where his father had been a distinguished member of the college football team.

After college Young played for a couple of other teams before joining the San Francisco 49ers in 1987 as backup to much-loved quarterback Joe Montana. His first years in San Francisco were not easy—some people were cold to him because they thought he was trying to replace Montana. But when Montana's career ended it was Young's turn in the spotlight. "I decided I just had to be me and play ball," he says of that period, and after a season or two he began winning fans of his own. Young was soon recognized as the most accurate passer in the eighty-year history of the National Football League (NFL) and earned wide admiration for being able to carry the ball as well as throw it. He took plenty of hard knocks on the football field, but he also set a number of NFL records and led his team to many victories. The sweetest victory was in January 1995, when the 49ers defeated the San Diego Chargers to win the Super Bowl. With quiet determination, Steve Young had become a football legend.

6 UTAH
ROAD TRIP

As she planned her family's vacation in Utah, Sue Munro of Atlanta, Georgia, looked at her stack of maps and brochures and said, "The real question isn't 'Where do you start?' It's 'How many weeks have you got?'" The Munros started in Salt Lake City. You might do the same on your own road trip around the Beehive State.

AROUND SALT LAKE CITY

Temple Square, one of the oldest parts of Salt Lake City, houses the major structures of the Church of Jesus Christ of Latter-day Saints. The square is a place of pilgrimage for Mormons, but many non-Mormons enjoy touring its beautifully maintained gardens and buildings, including the tabernacle. Only the temple itself is closed to the public. In and around the square you can also see monuments to the seagulls and the handcart pioneers that played important roles in early Mormon history and visit the Beehive House, Brigham Young's restored residence. Temple Square is always full of young Mormons, who are eager to answer questions and show visitors around.

Backed by broad mountains that are speckled green with trees and white with snow, Salt Lake City is a handsome place. It's also easy to tour on foot or bicycle. Climb uphill to the state capitol for a wide view of the city, and admire the building's copper dome and the

Salt Lake's Mormon temple, the center of a worldwide faith, anchors Temple Square, the heart of the state capital.

thirty-eight varieties of trees on the grounds. Inside you'll find murals illustrating key eras and events in the state's history. Leaving the capitol, look in on the Utah State Historical Museum, located in an old railroad station, or the Pioneer Memorial Museum, which is a duplicate of the Salt Lake Theater, an ornate showplace from pioneer days.

Before leaving the vicinity of Salt Lake City, check out the lake itself. Depending upon the light, the water appears blue, green,

TEN LARGEST CITIES

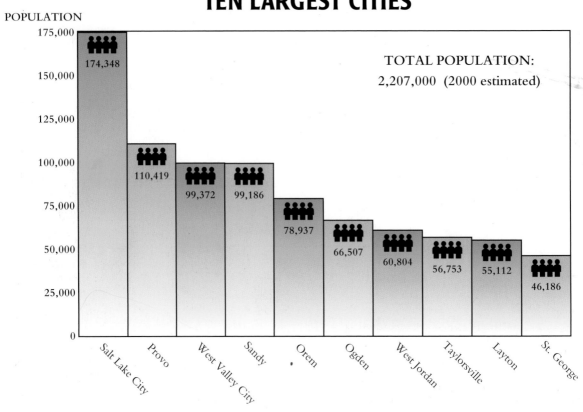

PLACES TO SEE

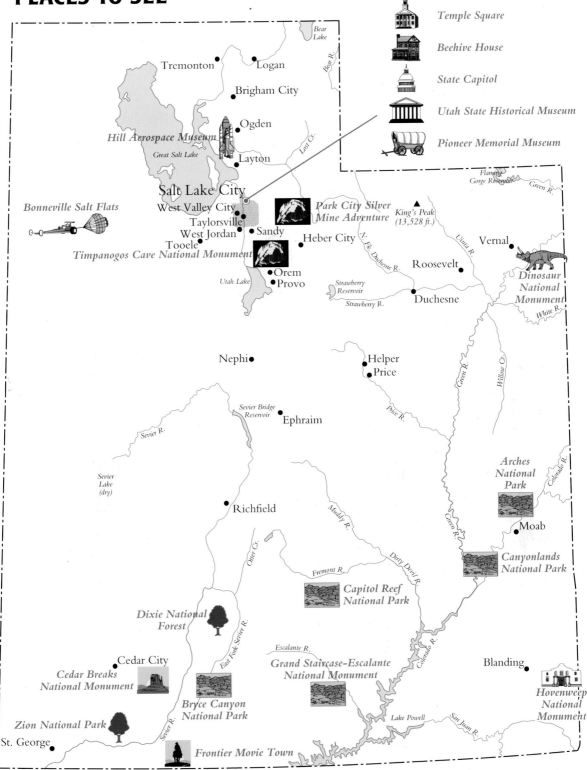

Temple Square

Beehive House

State Capitol

Utah State Historical Museum

Pioneer Memorial Museum

Bear Lake

Tremonton

Logan

Brigham City

Ogden

Hill Aerospace Museum

Great Salt Lake

Layton

Lost Cr.

Bear R.

Salt Lake City

West Valley City

Taylorsville

Bonneville Salt Flats

West Jordan

Sandy

Tooele

Timpanogos Cave National Monument

Heber City

Park City Silver Mine Adventure

▲ *King's Peak (13,528 ft.)*

N. Fk. Duchesne R.

Uinta R.

Vernal

Dinosaur National Monument

Roosevelt

White R.

Orem
Provo

Utah Lake

Strawberry Reservoir

Duchesne

Strawberry R.

Flaming Gorge Reservoir

Green R.

Nephi

Helper
Price

Green R.

Willow Cr.

Sevier Bridge Reservoir

Ephraim

Price R.

Sevier R.

Sevier Lake (dry)

Richfield

Muddy R.

Arches National Park

Colorado R.

Moab

Otter Cr.

Fremont R.

Capitol Reef National Park

Dirty Devil R.

Green R.

Canyonlands National Park

Dixie National Forest

East Fork Sevier R.

Cedar City

Escalante R.

Grand Staircase-Escalante National Monument

Colorado R.

Blanding

Cedar Breaks National Monument

Bryce Canyon National Park

Sevier R.

Lake Powell

San Juan R.

Hovenweep National Monument

Zion National Park

St. George

Frontier Movie Town

gray, or even maroon—its mineral content gives it strange colors. Antelope Island has beaches where you can take a dip. An Oregon couple who did so had two common reactions. One of them exclaimed, "Cool! Look how I'm floating!" The other cried, "Eww! There are little critters in this water, and it's slimy!" Rinse in fresh water as soon as you get out, or you'll itch from the salt for the rest of the day.

When you leave Salt Lake City you may head west for a look at the salt desert and the wide-open spaces of the Basin and Range

A crumbling movie set once recreated the Old West in Paria Canyon, near Kanab.

province. Or you may go northeast to explore mountain towns, green valleys, and the wilderness areas of the Rocky Mountain province. Most visitors, however, head south to Utah's most dramatic geology and its string of five national parks (only California and Alaska have more). On the way, stop at Timpanogos Cave National Monument. You'll hike a mile and a half up a mountain to reach the cave, but the climb is scenic and the monument is even better. It consists of three caves linked by narrow tunnels and draped in an amazing variety of crystals and dripstone formations. At forty-five degrees, the cave is a chilly relief on a hot summer day.

As you drive through Utah, it may seem familiar, and no wonder—the state's landscapes have served as the background for dozens of television shows and movies. If you can't get to Utah, you can see it in such films as the John Wayne classic *Stagecoach*, as well as *Planet of the Apes*, *Butch Cassidy and the Sundance Kid*, and *Independence Day*.

THE SOUTHEAST

Head for Moab, set amid hundreds of square miles of the smoothly curving, polished red sandstone known as slickrock. At Arches National Park you can hike among enormous rock formations, including more than 1,500 natural arches, the remnants of rock walls that have worn away from beneath due to weathering. Nowhere in the world can you see more rock arches than in this place. Hike a little way along one of the trails in the late afternoon, and then sit in the desert silence and watch the sunset illuminate red rock against a deep blue sky.

BURNING UP THE SALT FLATS

The Native Americans, early explorers, and pioneers who shunned the Great Salt Desert would be astonished to see how part of it is used today. Near the town of Wendover, an extremely flat, level area of the desert covering about one hundred square miles is known as the Bonneville Salt Flats. Since the early days of automobiles, drivers have found the smooth, hard salt flats an ideal surface for racing. Hundreds of land speed records for cars and motorcycles have been set on the ten-mile circular course called the Bonneville Speedway or on straight stretches of the flats themselves.

In 1947 at Bonneville, British driver John Cobb became the first person to travel on land at more than 400 miles per hour. Another Briton, John Noble, set a new record of 633.5 miles per hour in a jet-powered car in 1983. He and other superfast drivers are confident that sometime in the early twenty-first century someone will break the sound barrier—about 750 miles per hour—in a car. That milestone might take place at Bonneville, one of the few places on Earth with flat, straight, unobstructed courses long enough to allow jet-engine cars to speed up and slow down safely. "This empty, useless wasteland," as one U.S. Army surveyor called it in the 1850s, turned out to be good for something after all!

A backpacker heads out on a hike among the vivid red formations at Arches National Park.

Moving southwest from Moab you'll reach Canyonlands National Park, which the Indians called Land of Standing Stones. In the area known as Island in the Sky you'll drive across a high, narrow rock bridge called the Neck onto a peninsula that overlooks a dizzying panorama of canyons, cliffs, spires, and buttes. Far below, too deep in their canyons to be seen, the Green and Colorado Rivers meet. Explorer John Wesley Powell passed this spot in 1869 when he led the first expedition ever to float down the Green and the lower Colorado. No doubt he would be amazed to see the rubber rafts that carry tourists through those surging waters today.

Your next stop is the Needles district of Canyonlands National Park, a "weird sandstone forest," in one travel writer's words, of sharp red-rock pinnacles. Deep in the park, at Cave Spring, you'll find traces of human presence—battered wooden furniture made and left under a rock overhang by cowboys who herded cattle here in the early twentieth century.

Swing farther south and follow a dirt road to Hovenweep National Monument, the largest set of Anasazi ruins in this part of the Four Corners. Hovenweep was once a thriving community, but now it is just what its name means in the Ute language: "deserted valley." To the west is another national monument, Natural Bridges. It has three of the world's largest rock bridges (unlike arches, bridges are formed by streams flowing underneath).

Heading west, you must cross Glen Canyon, now filled with the backed-up waters of the Colorado River. There are two ways of crossing, a bridge and a ferry. Both offer dramatic views of cliffs, water, and pleasure boats cruising the Colorado. On the other side of Glen Canyon you'll move toward the third in southern Utah's necklace of national parks, Capitol Reef. Along the way, the road passes one of the few human monuments in this vast landscape. A tiny stone cabin at the dusty bottom of a cliff is all that remains of the 1882 homestead of Elijah Behunin and his family of ten.

Theirs must have been a hard life—the cabin was so small that the Behunin boys slept in caves in the cliff.

Capitol Reef gets its name from a huge rock formation that, from some angles, resembles the dome of the Capitol in Washington, D.C. The park lies along a one-hundred-mile fold in the earth's surface. Because pools of rainwater sometimes form in bowl-shaped depressions along this steep wrinkle, it is called the Waterpocket Fold. The pools sustain wildlife ranging from spadefoot toads to bighorn sheep and bobcats. A twenty-four-mile road lets you experience a bit of the

After camping along the San Juan River in Glen Canyon National Recreation Area, rafters prepare to ride the river for another day.

Rainpools like this one, held in the Capitol Reef's Waterpocket Fold, support bird, animal, and insect life through the hot summer days.

park from your car, but, as a park ranger puts it, "Capitol Reef is really a getting-out-there-and-backpacking kind of place." A restored one-room log schoolhouse in the park is a relic of Fruita, a former Mormon community. After the park was created in 1937 the people moved away, but the orchards they had planted still bear fruit.

THE SOUTHWEST

West of Capitol Reef you'll enter the High Plateau Mountains on a road that climbs into the Dixie National Forest. The tall trees and green grass are cool and refreshing after so many miles of rock. Two New Yorkers vacationing in Utah decided to camp overnight in the forest. "I'm a little tired of geology right now," one confessed. "I'm just happy to see dirt, grass, and trees."

Coming down out of the forest, you'll skirt the northern edge of Grand Staircase–Escalante National Monument. A few stunning canyons and arches can be visited by car along the fringe of this vast expanse, but real exploration requires backcountry hiking. Be warned—this monument is not for the inexperienced or unprepared. "Canyon country navigation is quite difficult," said Jim Sharp of Colorado after a three-day adventure. "There were a few times when I thought I wouldn't make it out."

On the western edge of Grand Staircase–Escalante lies Utah's fourth national park, Bryce Canyon. It consists of a series of breaks, or semicircular bowls like amphitheaters, that erosion has carved into a two-thousand-foot pink cliff. Stand on the edge of the cliff and look out and down into the breaks at thousands of pink-and-white hoodoos marching into the distance. Or hike a trail down into the hoodoo forest—and back up again, of course. By sunlight Bryce Canyon is a magnificent wonderland of color. By moonlight it is a mysterious, whimsical maze. It is also, said Ebenezer Bryce, who ranched in the canyon in the late nineteenth century, "a hell of a place to lose a cow."

Zion National Park in Utah's southwest corner is the opposite of Bryce. Instead of standing high on a rim looking down into the park, you'll enter a deep, narrow canyon between towering vertical walls and crane your neck to look up at their domed tops. Native Americans would not live in the canyon—they found it too dark and ominous when evening shadows fell. Today Zion is one of the most visited parks in the nation, although relatively few people make the all-day effort to climb the trails that lead up the three-thousand-foot cliffs.

Before leaving southern Utah, stop in at least one more of its engaging towns. You could visit the busy southern city of St. George, which has the oldest Mormon Temple still standing in Utah. "Utah's summer spends the winter in St. George," boast townsfolk proud of the mild winter weather. Brigham Young must have agreed—he spent his winters in St. George, where you can now tour the house he built around 1873.

Another colorful stop in southern Utah is Kanab, gateway to the North Rim of Arizona's Grand Canyon. So many movie and television Westerns have been filmed around Kanab that locals call the place Little Hollywood. One of the most used movie sets is the Wild West main street that runs through Old Paria, a few miles east of Kanab.

If you have time for one more spectacular sight, and if you still

This rock formation, one of hundreds of thousands in Bryce Canyon National Park, is called Thor's Hammer, after the weapon wielded by one of the gods of Norse mythology.

haven't had enough geology, go to Cedar Breaks National Monument, which one ranger calls "Utah's best spot that no one visits."
Like Bryce Canyon but smaller and higher, Cedar Breaks is a string
of red-rock amphitheaters. Its rim is 10,000 feet above sea level,
so high that in some years snow closes the road until midsummer,

and a chill wind constantly buffets the 2,500-foot-deep breaks. Perched between Utah's high country and its western deserts, Cedar Breaks is as wild and beautiful as anything in the state, a good place to say farewell to "the land no one wanted."

An explosion of brilliant color and raw rock high atop a plateau, Cedar Breaks is sometimes overshadowed by Utah's larger and more famous parks. One visitor said, "If Cedar Breaks were anywhere but this region, it would be picked as one of the world's greatest scenic wonders."

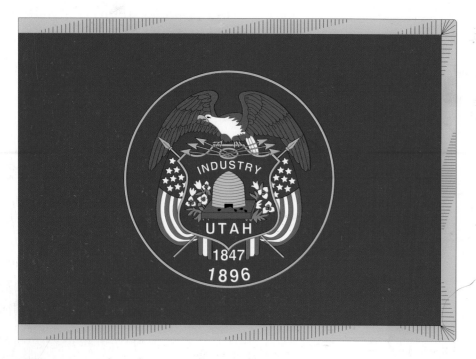

THE FLAG: *Adopted in 1913, the state flag shows the state seal with a yellow border.*

THE SEAL: *Utah's seal, which was approved in 1896, shows a bald eagle, representing protection, atop a beehive, representing hard work. The hive is surrounded by sego lilies, which stand for peace. Above the beehive is the word* Industry, *the state motto; below it are the dates 1847, the year the first Mormons arrived in Utah, and 1896, the year Utah became a state.*

STATE SURVEY

Statehood: January 4, 1896

Origin of Name: From the Ute Indians, whose name means "people of the mountains"

Nickname: Beehive State

Capital: Salt Lake City

Motto: Industry

Insect: Honeybee

Bird: California seagull

Flower: Sego lily

Tree: Blue spruce

Animal: Rocky Mountain elk

Fish: Bonneville cutthroat trout

Gem: Topaz

Grass: Indian rice grass

California seagull

Sego lily

UTAH, WE LOVE THEE

Evan Stephens arrived in Salt Lake City on October 2, 1866, having crossed the plains with his parents in a covered wagon. He conducted the Mormon Tabernacle Choir from 1890 to 1916. He wrote this song in 1917. It was adopted as the official state song in 1937.

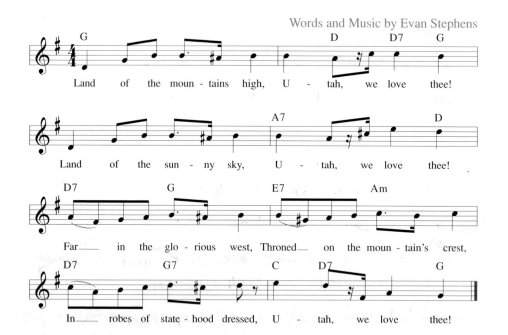

Words and Music by Evan Stephens

Fruit: Cherry

Mineral: Copper

Fossil: Allosaurus

GEOGRAPHY

Highest Point: 13,528 feet above sea level, at Kings Peak

Lowest Point: 2,000 feet above sea level, at Beaver Dam Creek in Washington County

Area: 84,905 square miles

Greatest Distance, North to South: 342 miles

Greatest Distance, East to West: 276 miles

Bordering States: Idaho to the north, Wyoming to the northeast, Colorado to the east, Arizona to the south, Nevada to the west

Hottest Recorded Temperature: 117°F in St. George on July 5, 1985

Coldest Recorded Temperature: -69°F at Peter's Sink on February 1, 1985

Average Annual Precipitation: 12 inches

Major Rivers: Bear, Colorado, Green, Provo, Sevier, Snake, Weber

Major Lakes: Bear, Clear, Great Salt, Powell, Utah

Trees: aspen, balsam, birch, box elder, cottonwood, fir, juniper, mesquite, pine, spruce, sycamore, willow

Wild Plants: creosote, greasewood, Indian paintbrush, lupine, prickly pear, sagebrush, yucca

Animals: badger, black bear, bobcat, coyote, elk, fox, lynx, marten, mountain lion, mule deer, muskrat, porcupine, rabbit, scorpion, skunk

Mountain lion

Birds: duck, eagle, goose, grouse, heron, owl, pheasant, quail, seagull, titmouse

Fish: bass, carp, catfish, grayling, perch, trout, whitefish

Endangered Animals: black-footed ferret, bonytail chub, Colorado squaw-fish, humpback chub, June sucker, Kanab ambersnail, razorback sucker, Southwestern willow flycatcher, Utah valvata snail, Virgin River chub, whooping crane, woundfin

Black-footed ferret

Endangered Plants: autumn buttercup, Barneby reed-mustard, Barneby ridge-cress, clay phacelia, dwarf bear-poppy, Kodachrome bladderpod, San Rafael cactus, shrubby reed-mustard, Wright fishhook cactus

TIMELINE

Utah History

1500s The Gosiute, Paiute, Ute, Navajo, and Shoshone Indians live in present-day Utah

1765 Spaniard Juan Antonio Rivera becomes the first European known to enter Utah

1776 Silvestre Vélez de Escalante and Francisco Domínguez travel from Santa Fe, New Mexico, to Utah Lake in search of a route to California

1824–1825 Jim Bridger is likely the first white person to see the Great Salt Lake

1841 The first wagon train of settlers crosses Utah on the way to California

1847 The first Mormons reach Utah

1848 The United States gains possession of Utah from Mexico

1850 Utah Territory is established; the *Deseret News*, Utah's first newspaper, begins publication in Salt Lake City; the University of Deseret, which is later renamed the University of Utah, is founded

1852 Brigham Young, the president of the Mormon Church, publicly endorses polygamy

1856–1860 Three thousand Mormons haul their possessions to Utah in what is known as the Handcart Migration

1857 President James Buchanan sends troops to Utah to enforce his appointment of the territorial governor, resulting in the short-lived Utah War

1861 Telegraph lines meet in Salt Lake City, connecting the East and West Coasts

1862 Congress passes a law against polygamy

1863 U.S. troops massacre more than 200 Shoshones in the Battle of Bear River

1866 Utah's first free public school opens in American Fork

1867 The Mormon Tabernacle is completed

1868 Corrine, the first non-Mormon town in Utah, is founded

1869 The first railroad line across the United States is completed at Promontory Point

1890 Utah establishes free public schools; the leader of the Mormon Church advises Mormons to give up polygamy

1896 Utah becomes the 45th state

1897 The state legislature passes a law establishing free public libraries

1900 Two hundred people are killed in a mine explosion in Scofield

1915 Labor leader Joe Hill is convicted of murder and executed, making headlines around the world

1917–1918 The United States engages in World War I

1922 Utah's first radio station, KZN, begins broadcasting in Salt Lake City

1941–1945 Ten military bases are built in Utah during World War II

1964 Flaming Gorge and Glen Canyon Dams are completed, creating Flaming Gorge Reservoir and Lake Powell

2002 Salt Lake City hosts the winter Olympics

ECONOMY

Agricultural Products: apples, barley, beef cattle, eggs, greenhouse and nursery plants, hay, hogs, milk, pears, potatoes, sheep, turkeys, wheat

Manufactured Products: aluminum, food products, medical instruments, newspapers, steel, transportation equipment

Natural Resources: coal, copper, gold, magnesium, natural gas, petroleum, salt, silver, uranium

Business and Trade: banking, engineering, insurance, real estate, tourism, wholesale and retail trade

Coal mining

CALENDAR OF CELEBRATIONS

Sundance Film Festival Independent films by young filmmakers are the focus of this world-famous festival in Park City each January.

Snowshine Festival With events such as snow softball and family ski races, this March festival in Park City is fun for the whole family.

Mountain Man Rendezvous Every April in Ogden men and women wearing skins and furs demonstrate their skill at leatherwork, musket shooting, and cooking over a Dutch oven.

Last Spike Ceremony Each May 10, costumed actors at the Golden Spike National Historic Site in Brigham City reenact the driving of the golden spike that completed the first railroad across the United States.

Living Traditions Festival Singers and dancers representing the many ethnic groups that have made Salt Lake City what it is celebrate their heritage at this May event.

Scandinavian Festival Each May, Ephraim revels in its Scandinavian background with lots of traditional food, music, dancing, and crafts.

Northern Ute Fourth of July Pow Wow People from all over the West travel to Fort Duchesne on the Uintah and Ouray Indian Reservation each July to enjoy the dance competitions, rodeo, and crafts exhibits.

Days of '47 The first Mormons arrived in the Salt Lake City region in July 1847. Each year, the city celebrates this event with concerts, fireworks, the state's largest rodeo, and one of the nation's largest parades.

Festival of the American West Utah's pioneer past is remembered in Logan during late July and early August with two weeks of mock shootouts, cowboy poetry, square dancing, and panning for gold.

Festival of the American West

Timpanogos Storytelling Festival Everyone enjoys the spellbinding tales woven by the talented storytellers who travel to Orem for this August event.

Melon Days The tiny town of Green River honors its tasty cantaloupes and watermelons with a September celebration that features a parade, square dancing, and free melons of all kinds.

Greek Festival Lively dancing, rich food, and a tour of Salt Lake City's Holy Trinity Greek Orthodox Cathedral are all part of this September celebration.

Canyonlands Fat Tire Festival Utahns celebrate one of their favorite sports—mountain biking—in Moab each October with guided tours, hill climbs, and workshops.

Christmas Village A parade and tree-lighting ceremony in late November kick off Christmastime in Ogden, when the municipal park comes alive with thousands of tiny lights and animated figures.

STATE STARS

Hal Ashby (1936–1988), a film director, was born in Ogden. Ashby first earned acclaim as a film editor, winning an Academy Award in 1967 for *In the Heat of the Night*. He made his directing debut in 1970 with *The Landlord*. Ashby soon developed a reputation for making oddly humorous films, such as *Harold and Maude*, the story of the relationship between a feisty old woman and a teenage boy obsessed with death. He also directed such popular films as *Shampoo*, *Being There*, and *Coming Home*.

Roseanne Barr (1952–   ), an actor and comedian known for her irreverent and sometimes abrasive humor, was born in Salt Lake City. She was a housewife and mother of three when she began doing stand-up comedy

in 1981. Her aggressive routines about being a housewife soon earned her national attention. In 1988 she began appearing in her own television show, *Roseanne*, in which she played a feisty working-class mother. She has also appeared in movies, written two books, and hosted her own talk show.

Roseanne Barr

Jim Bridger (1804–1881), one of the most famous mountain men, was likely the first white man to see the Great Salt Lake. Bridger, who was born in Virginia, joined his first fur-trapping expedition in 1822. In the following decades he often served as a guide and scout, so that over his lifetime, he explored much of the West.

Jim Bridger

John Browning (1855–1926) was perhaps the most successful inventor of firearms in American history. Browning, who began working in his father's gunsmith shop while still a child, made his first gun when he was 13 years old. His most famous inventions were the Winchester repeating rifle and the Browning automatic rifle, both of which became standard in the U.S. Army. Browning was born in Provo.

Nolan Bushnell (1943–   ) invented Pong, the world's first video game. In 1972, the same year Pong went on the market, he also founded Atari, an early powerhouse in the video game market. Bushnell was born in Ogden and attended Utah State College and the University of Utah.

Nolan Bushnell

Jack Dempsey

Jack Dempsey (1895–1983) was the world heavyweight boxing champion from 1919 to 1926. Dempsey was born in Colorado and moved to Utah when he was a child. He first entered the ring in 1914 and in the next few years won almost every bout by a knockout. Dempsey was a powerful, relentless puncher and often defeated much larger men. He was elected to the International Boxing Hall of Fame in 1954.

Philo T. Farnsworth (1906–1971), the inventor of television, was born in Beaver. As a child, Farnsworth loved to tinker with things, and he won a national invention contest at age 13. He came up with the concept of television while still in high school and by age 21 had produced a working model. Farnsworth also developed the first simple electron microscope and an early type of radar. By his death, he had registered 300 patents, more than 100 of them related to television.

John Dennis Fitzgerald (1907–1988), a native of Price, was a beloved children's author, most famous for his Great Brain series. These humorous tales concern the adventures of two brothers—one of them a brilliant schemer—growing up in Utah a hundred years ago. Fitzgerald also wrote adult books, including the memoir *Papa Married a Mormon*, about his youth in Utah.

Orrin Hatch (1934–   ) has been a U.S. senator since 1977. Hatch was born in Pennsylvania, attended Brigham Young University, and became a lawyer in Salt Lake City. Although he had never before held elective office, he won election to the U.S. Senate in 1976. Since then, he has established himself as one of the Senate's leading conservative voices. He is the chairman of the powerful Judiciary Committee and also serves on the Finance Committee.

Orrin Hatch

"Big Bill" Haywood (1869–1928), a native of Salt Lake City, was one of the most famous labor leaders of the early 20th century. Haywood became a miner at age 15 and eventually led the Western Federation of Miners. He also helped found the Industrial Workers of the World, a radical labor organization. In 1918 he was convicted of crimes against the state for opposing U.S. efforts in World War I. To avoid prison, he fled to Russia, which was then the communist nation called the Soviet Union. He is one of only two Americans buried in the Kremlin, the heart of the Russian government.

J. Willard Marriott (1900–1985) founded the Marriott Corporation, which runs hundreds of hotels and restaurants. He was born in the town of Marriott, which was named after his grandfather, who had taken part in the 1847 Mormon migration to Utah. While attending the University of Utah, Marriott opened a root beer stand. In 1927, he decided a root beer stand would thrive in Washington, D.C., because of the hot summers, so he started one there. Soon, he expanded the menu to include hot food, and the restaurants began multiplying. In 1957, he opened the first Marriott Hotel. Marriott continued as president of the Marriott Corporation until 1964.

Merlin Olsen (1940–   ), one of the all-time great football linemen, was born in Logan. Olsen was an All-American player at Utah State University. He joined the Los Angeles Rams in 1962 and won Rookie of the Year honors. Both powerful and smart, he eventually played in a record 14 Pro Bowl games in a row. After retiring from football, Olsen became an actor, appearing on such television programs as *Little House on the Prairie* and *Father Murphy*. He also works as a sports announcer. Olsen was inducted into the Pro Football Hall of Fame in 1982.

Merlin Olsen

Harold Ross (1892–1951) was the founding editor of the prestigious magazine the *New Yorker*. Born in Colorado, he moved to Salt Lake City when he was very young. Ross became interested in journalism in high school, and in 1906 he became an apprentice reporter for the *Salt Lake City Tribune*. He worked for a variety of newspapers before cofounding the *New Yorker* in 1925. The magazine quickly became famous for its wit, sophistication, and excellent writers and cartoonists. Ross himself was renowned for his precise editing and remarkable literary judgment.

Jedediah Strong Smith (1799–1831) was the first white man to travel the length and breadth of Utah. Smith, a New York native, was a fur trapper and explorer. In 1826 he became the first American to enter California from the east. He also helped open up the coastal trading route from California to Oregon.

Jedediah Strong Smith

Virginia Sorensen (1912–1991), who wrote books for both children and adults, was born in Provo and grew up in Manti. Her works for children include *The House Next Door*, about a teenage girl living in Salt Lake City a century ago, and *Miracles on Maple Hill*, about a city girl who moves to a farmhouse, which earned the Newbery Medal in 1957 for best children's book.

Wallace Stegner (1909–1993) was a leading writer about the West and the environment. Stegner was born in Iowa but moved to Utah as a child. He attended the University of Utah, where he also taught. His writings include *The Gathering of Zion*, a history of the Mormon Trail, and *Angle of Repose*, a Pulitzer Prize–winning novel about a man looking into the lives of his pioneer grandparents. Stegner won the National Book Award in 1977 for his novel *The Spectator Bird*, which concerns the memories of a literary agent.

May Swenson (1919–1989) was a renowned poet noted for her precise imagery. She was born in Logan and attended Utah State University. Her poetry collections include *Another Animal*, *A Cage of Spines*, and *To Mix with Time*. She also wrote three books of poetry for children, including *The Complete Poems to Solve*.

May Swenson

Brigham Young (1801–1877) was the second president of the Mormon Church. Young, who was born in Vermont, converted to Mormonism in 1832. When Joseph Smith, the founder of Mormonism, was killed, Young took over as head of the church. He directed the migration of thousands of Mormons to Utah beginning in 1847. He founded Salt Lake City and oversaw the establishment of more than 350 Mormon towns. When Utah became a U.S. territory in 1850, he was appointed territorial governor. Although Young ceased being governor after 1857, he remained president of the church until his death.

Loretta Young (1914–   ), a beautiful actress from Salt Lake City, made almost a hundred films in the 1930s and 1940s. Young, who projected a wholesome image, became famous for such films as *Platinum Blonde* and *The Stranger*. In 1947 she won an Academy Award for her performance in *The Farmer's Daughter,* as a Swedish immigrant who starts out a maid and ends up a congresswoman. In the 1950s she had her own television show, *The Loretta Young Show*, for which she won three Emmy Awards.

Loretta Young

Steve Young (1961–) is the most accurate passer in football history. He began setting records when he was still the quarterback at Brigham Young University. As the quarterback for the San Francisco 49ers, he led the National Football League (NFL) in passing four years in a row, a new record. He was named NFL Player of the Year twice and threw a record six touchdowns in the 1995 Super Bowl. Young, a great-great-great grandson of Brigham Young, was born in Salt Lake City.

TOUR THE STATE

Miles Goodyear Cabin (Ogden) The oldest non-Indian building in Utah, this tiny cabin was built in 1845 from cottonwood logs.

Hill Aerospace Museum (Roy) At this museum, you can get a close-up view of all sorts of military aircraft, including the B-17 and the SR-71. You can also see flight simulators, jet engines, and a restored barracks from World War II.

Antelope Island State Park (Syracuse) Floating is so easy in the Great Salt Lake, you'll feel like you can walk on water. Antelope Island, which lies seven miles out in the lake, is also a great place for hiking and wildlife viewing—you might even see buffalo!

Mormon Tabernacle (Salt Lake City) This dome-shaped building where the Mormon Tabernacle Choir sings is famed for its amazing acoustics and its gigantic pipe organ, which has more than 12,000 pipes.

Wheeler Historic Farm (Salt Lake City) Gather eggs, milk cows, and take a hayride at this re-creation of a farm from the beginning of the 20th century.

Pioneer Memorial Museum (Salt Lake City) This fun museum displays everything from quilts to a mule-drawn streetcar.

Alta Ski Area (Alta) Glide down the slopes at one of the world's best ski areas, famed for its powdery snow.

Heber Valley Historic Railroad (Heber City) Antique trains take visitors into Provo Canyon all the way to Vivian Park, the perfect place for a picnic.

John Hutchings Museum of Natural History (Lehi) You'll see fossils, Indian arts, unusual rocks, and much more at this wide-ranging collection.

Timpanogos Cave National Monument (American Fork) Few caves are as colorful as this one located high in a scenic canyon. It is packed with formations, some of them light shades of green, yellow, and red.

McCurdy Historical Doll Museum (Provo) About 3,000 dolls are housed in this unusual museum. They range from Hopi kachinas to figures of presidents.

Goblin Valley (Green River) A favorite pastime among young and old alike in Utah is running and hiding among the oddly shaped formations in this park. Some look like toadstools, some like goblins, others like little babies.

Flaming Gorge National Recreation Area (Dutch John) Boaters, swimmers, fishers, and waterskiers all love this site. You can also enjoy some gorgeous hikes and take an elevator 500 feet down into the Flaming Gorge Dam, where you can see the giant turbines and generators that transform the flowing water of the Green River into electricity.

Dinosaur National Monument (Jensen) Many of the dinosaur skeletons on display at natural history museums around the country have been found at this spot, where you can watch scientists slowly unearth fossilized dinosaur bones.

Dinosaur National Monument

Arches National Park (Moab) On a visit to this park, you'll be surrounded by more than 2,000 red sandstone arches, from tiny to towering.

Newspaper Rock (Moab) Everyone from the Anasazi to Mormon pioneers has scratched pictures and designs into the soft surface of this rock.

Canyonlands National Park (Moab) Check out the fantastic views at Island in the Sky or wander through the red-rock spires of the Needles district at this sprawling park.

Hovenweep National Monument (Bluff) The Anasazi Indians constructed the massive buildings at this monument 800 years ago. One of the most interesting ruins is Square Tower, which experts believe may have been used as an observatory.

Bryce Canyon National Park (Bryce Canyon) You can explore colorful lime-stone formations, hike through cool forests, or snowshoe through the silence in the dead of winter at this fantastic national park.

Frontier Movie Town (Kanab) Many Westerns were filmed in Kanab, where you can visit some of the buildings that served as sets and see displays of movie memorabilia.

Coral Pink Sand Dunes State Park (Kanab) You'll feel like you're on another planet when you're in the middle of this vast sea of pink sand.

Zion National Park (Springdale) With its towering cliffs, deep chasms, spectacular hiking trails, and lovely waterfalls, Zion National Park has something to satisfy everyone.

FUN FACTS

The largest natural stone bridge in the world is Utah's Rainbow Bridge National Monument. It soars to a height of 290 feet and is 275 feet across.

When Martha Hughes Cannon was elected to the Utah state senate in 1896, it made headlines across the nation for two reasons. Not only had she become the country's first female state senator, but she had defeated her own husband in the election.

In 1912 voters in Kanab made history when they elected a woman to serve as mayor and four more women to fill all the positions on the town's board, creating the first all-female city government in the nation's history.

FIND OUT MORE

If you'd like to learn more about Utah, look for the titles below in your local library or bookstore. The websites listed at the end offer information and links to other resources.

GENERAL STATE BOOKS

Fradin, Dennis. *Utah*. Chicago: Children's Press, 1997.

Sirvaitis, Karen. *Utah*. Minneapolis: Lerner Publications, 1996.

Thompson, Kathleen. *Utah*. Austin, TX: Raintree/Steck-Vaughn, 1996.

SPECIAL INTEREST BOOKS

Fitzgerald, John D. *The Great Brain*. New York: Yearling, 1972.

———. *Me and My Little Brain*. New York: Yearling, 1972.

McPherson, Stephanie. *TV's Forgotten Hero: The Story of Philo Farnsworth*. Minneapolis: Carolrhoda Books, 1996.

Powell, Alan K. *Utah History Encyclopedia*. Salt Lake City: University of Utah Press, 1994.

Rambeck, Richard. *Utah Jazz*. Mankato, MN: Creative Education, 1998.

Swenson, May. *The Complete Poems to Solve.* New York: Macmillan, 1993.

Wharton, Gayen, and Tom Wharton. *It Happened in Utah.* Helena, MT: Falcon Publishing, 1998.

VIDEOS

Arches National Park. Finley-Holiday Film Corp., 1994.

Bryce Canyon. International Video Network, 1992.

The Geological and Natural History of Arches National Park. U-Matic, 1994.

A People's History of Utah. KUED-TV, 1988.

The State Parks in Utah. Media Entertainment.

Utah's Green River: A Wilderness Experience. Econews.

Zion National Park. Finley-Holiday Film Corp., 1994.

CD-ROMS

Southwestern Trails. Infomagic.

U.S. Geography: The Rockies. Dallas: ZCI Publishing, 1994.

WEBSITES

www.state.ut.us/ The official website of the state.

www.go-utah.com A travel and recreation guide.

INDEX

Page numbers for illustrations are in boldface.